Hidden SCARS

Hidden SCARS

Tattoos on the Soul

Tessa Rey

authorHOUSE®

AuthorHouse™
1663 Liberty Drive
Bloomington, IN 47403
www.authorhouse.com
Phone: 1-800-839-8640

Published by AuthorHouse   12/17/2012

ISBN: 978-1-4817-0007-8 (sc)
ISBN: 978-1-4817-0006-1 (hc)
ISBN: 978-1-4817-0005-4 (e)

Library of Congress Control Number: 2012923822

CONTENTS

CHAPTER 1

OPEN WOUNDS

It has been said, "Time heals all wounds." I do not agree. The wounds remain. In time, the mind, protecting its sanity, covers them with scar tissue and the pain lessens but is never gone.

—Rose Kennedy

As I stare into the mirror and examine the scars running across my chest and back, I am thankful I can hide them with clothes, but like physical scars that knot up over time and cause extreme pain, I am aware of the emotional scars that will also knot up and cause pain when they are pushed down and ignored over time.

I wanted to share my journey with you as I walked through the cleansing process of dealing with the emotional scars and acknowledging the physical ones. My transformation is here for you to witness, and I pray it might inspire some of you to always have hope and never give up.

As I wrote the following story and had to deal with the scars, I slowly began to heal in some areas and realized I just needed to let things go in other parts of my life. Love should never be conditional, and I have become aware that I spent my life looking for and trying to earn people's love. Then I discovered God's love (or agape love), and my life has never been the same.

As the title states, this book is about dealing with hidden scars, so I focused on the hurtful things; however, my life has been blessed with many wonderful moments as well. I learned that when something terrible happens, something amazing will also happen. I just have to find the joy in whatever is happening and enjoy my glass not only being half full but also overflowing. I also understand that because of my own pain, I have caused many scars to others as well, and I pray they will forgive me.

At the end of each chapter, I have included a sidenote with information on where one can find help with what I have experienced.

The names have been changed to protect identities.

I am a warrior. I don't know at what point in my life I learned how to overcome my adversities. I was small for my age, and people always told me I couldn't do things. It became a challenge. The tougher things were, the more I would push to overcome the obstacles. It took many years of slipping in the pit of life before I finally took hold of the Lord's outstretched hand and let Him pull me up out of the muck of life. Now I cannot believe I lived so long in that disgusting mess before I grabbed hold. People call me a survivor and an inspiration, but to me, a survivor is someone who has overcome their obstacles and lived to tell about it. I see myself as a warrior because my battles rage on. This is my story.

Childhood innocence must come to an end, and for some, it is much earlier than it is for others. My innocence was taken from me at eleven years of age. I was asleep in bed with my baby brother, Mark, tucked under my arm down the hall from our parents' bedroom, where we were awakened by their return late one night. I could tell Dad had been drinking again when his voice turned abusive toward Mom and he started beating on her. It was all I could do to keep Mark from running to them and so placed my hand over his mouth to stifle his cries. We both would flinch with each slap and whimper. I was terrified we would anger Dad and he would also hurt us. Until then, he had never laid a hand on either of us, but I had never seen this side of him. He had spanked our older brother and sister, Matthew and Sunny, often with the razor strap, which hung ever-present just outside the bathroom door in the hallway between our bedroom and my parents'. He had never laid a hand on Mom until that night, and when it was over, I heard him tell her to go file for divorce because he could not promise that he wouldn't beat her again. I held Mark long into the night as tears slipped silently down my cheeks until he fell asleep and I drifted off. The next morning, I was late getting up, and as I came around the corner into the living room, there was Mom in her rocking chair with a bruised and swollen face and missing a tooth, holding Mark. Dad had gotten up early and left. Guilt swept over me that I hadn't attempted to stop my dad. I had just lain in bed, hiding like a coward paralyzed with fear.

The next time I witnessed his rage was on New Year's Eve when I was home babysitting my younger sister and brother, Aponi and Mark, and Dad arrived. He waited for Mom and my older sister, Faith, to get home, and as they came through the door, he jumped up and pinned Mom in a corner, who then told Faith to call the cops. Dad threatened to hurt Mom but didn't go beyond getting in her face and holding her in a viselike grip with his forearm around her neck. When the police officer arrived, I was asked who I wished to stay with, and out of fear, I told him my father. I figured my mom had the older three kids but my dad just had us, and if I went with my mom, then he would be all alone. The police officer sent mom and Faith off to a friend's house for the night, leaving us with our dad. He had all three of us crawl in bed with him. An eleven-year-old should never be put in a position to choose between parents, and worse, whatever I chose, Aponi and Mark had to follow. My father moved out, and the family managed the best we could with us three younger ones going and staying with him at our grandmother's on the weekends. I was in sixth grade at this time. Mom had been married before my father and had had my brother and two sisters, Matthew, Sunny, and Faith. Then she married my father, and my younger sister, Aponi, my brother, Mark, and I were added to the family.

3

In May, our dad took all three of us to a rodeo with his girlfriend, so any hopes of parents reconciling was coming to an end. Later that month, he ran across someone he had known earlier in life and started dating her. Opal had two children of her own. He had Mom file the divorce papers, and so it was final. We would never be a family again. He and Opal were married and brought a daughter, Shelby, into the world the following year.

Mom had been working for Boise Cascade, and toward the end of my seventh-grade year, she decided to move the family. So she transferred jobs in order to drive a road grader up in the mountains during the week and then come home on weekends. I and the two younger siblings spent the summer with our dad and his new family, and because both adults worked, it became my job to manage the five younger ones, prepare dinner, and clean house. One time after an exhausting day of babysitting, preparing a roast with potatoes and carrots in the oven, and dusting, I felt really accomplished and proud of myself. But then Opal came home and immediately started running her fingers across the end tables in the living room and showing me how I had missed spots when I had been dusting. I was so angry and started to talk back, but Dad interrupted me, telling me to put my shoes on and help him irrigate. The time at my dad's became more stressful, and as seasons changed, we visited less and less, my dad becoming a stranger.

Mom got a boyfriend. When she was not working in the mountains, she was with him, leaving Sunny to be our caretaker. We were unsupervised most of the time because Sunny was involved in sports and had a job. I was really close with my grandmother on my dad's side and had always enjoyed visiting her. After the divorce, my father's siblings insisted us kids were too much for their mother to handle, and so my visits became few and far between, even though Grandma would call and beg for me to come spend time with her. I was twelve years old when she passed during an afternoon nap, but I had learned a very valuable lesson. My grandmother had always told me that if I laughed, the world would laugh with me but that if I cried, I would cry alone. So I learned how to hide my tears behind a big smile. Around that same time, I had started drinking and gotten drunk after my eighth-grade year, and through the years to come, I would use the alcohol to numb the pain that life would soon throw at me. My sisters always had big parties with lots of alcohol that lasted for days, and after one of these parties, I had decided to try drinking.

While my parents were still together, we would go to my cousin's house, and the adults would go out. One time, Star, my stepcousin, admitted that she was terrified of her stepdad, Uncle Alvah. Star had us practice an escape route should he come home in a drunken, abusive mood. We practiced escaping out the window and rescuing my baby cousin and then sneaking to the car in the shed and pushing it till we got it out of earshot. I could not comprehend why Star was so frightened until one night when Mom was at the bar and everyone had gone to bed. Sometime in the night, I was awakened in extreme terror. Someone was lying behind me, pressed up against me, with his arm pinning me down as he groped me. I fought with everything I had and pushed him away and thankfully was on the edge of the bed so he lost balance and fell to the floor. At this point I realized it was Uncle Alvah. Once I freed his hand, he just got up and staggered out of the room. I noticed then that Aponi and Mark were also in Mom's bed with me. I lay there, once more feeling like a coward, too afraid to move while I listened to him go into Faith's room, where shortly after, I heard a slap and Faith cussing him out. Then I could hear him move down the hall and stairs to where Sunny was sleeping. He was down there for quite some time before he came back up and went out the door. I knew about the loaded gun in the closet and tried to still my nerves and get up, but the few strides may as well have been a hundred. I was too frozen with fright to move. Later, I found out Aponi had fallen asleep in the living room and Uncle Alvah had molested her first. She had gotten up and crawled in bed with me to hide from him, and he had followed her. I tried to tell Mom the next day, but she didn't want to hear it, and so my pleas fell on deaf ears. I came to believe that no one cared about what happened to me and that I would have to deal with these things on my own. All the adults in my life were too occupied with their own lives to show concern—except my grandma, and I had just lost her.

The summer after eighth grade, Mom moved the family back to our small hometown but sent Sunny and me ahead. We moved in with her parents and my Uncle Alvah, even after we had told her that he had molested all of her daughters in one night. One night while I was asleep on the living room floor in a sleeping bag, I was once again awakened by someone groping me. I fought with all my might and was able to get away. Then I curled up in the bottom of the sleeping bag, wrapping the zipper underneath. The worst part was that my grandfather had started talking dirty to me since we had moved back. He would expose himself when no one was around so I was not even sure if it was my uncle or grandfather who had touched me this time. They both smoked the same brand of cigarettes, and the air was just putrid with the smell. This experience triggered a terror that would be with me for many years to come. No one could touch me in the middle of the night when I was in a deep sleep without sending me into an anxiety attack. I told no one about this second incident because I figured I must have deserved the attention these men were giving me. I became a loner, not wanting to trust people but longing to be loved at the same time. I had a deep, desperate longing to feel loved.

We bounced between house rentals throughout my high school years but stayed around our hometown, and Uncle Alvah was there to go into drunken rages. One time, he shot at us while he was chasing our horses through the fields and threatening to shoot them. We had to get out of the van and hide behind it as bullets zinged past us. The summer following this incident, Uncle Alvah went to rehab, and everyone convinced us kids that he was safe to be around again because he no longer drank and had only been dangerous from drinking. So one day following my freshman year of high school, he stopped by the house and asked me to go with him to gather cattle up in the mountains. I was in charge of Aponi and Mark as usual, and so I told him I couldn't; however, Aponi volunteered, and I gave her permission. If there was one decision in my whole life I could take back, it would be this one. The next day, no one was waiting for me after driver's education, so I finally walked up town and called the house. My grandma answered. I was told my mom had to go get Aponi and that grandma would be in to get me shortly. I was furious I had been forgotten in town and was pouting pretty hard by the time Grandma arrived. When I got home, my older sister filled me in on Aponi, and the guilt that swept over me was overwhelming. I had left my baby sister wide open for such painful abuse. Uncle Alvah had showed up to get me, but instead, I had let Aponi take my place. Unknowingly to us, he had planned far ahead already, spiking orange juice with drugs and alcohol and then making her drink it. After she passed out, he abused her. The next morning when she awoke, he was sitting on his horse outside the tent, headed out to gather cattle, but he made sure to tell her what he had done before he rode off. Aponi waited till he was out of sight and ran all the way to town, ducking and hiding behind trees and running over hayfields that had just been mowed while she was barefoot, slicing her feet to shreds. She made it to town and got a drink of soda but started vomiting violently. She called our mom and hid until she arrived. Mom took her to the doctor, who confirmed she had been abused. When Aponi got home that night and I saw the shape her feet were in, the realization of what my little sister had endured just sickened me. The next year proved to devour the family, our grandmother posting Alvah's bail, and so we had loaded guns by the door with instructions to shoot him on the spot. Aponi testified, sending Uncle Alvah away to prison for ten years, but he escaped once and headed after our mom and Aponi. Thankfully, patrols stopped him before he reached the family. I had left for the US Air Force to escape; however, everyone continued to live in constant fear, and I would have nightmares for years to come. He was able to reach out to people from prison, and he threaten to kill or burn houses down, so he was required to serve his complete sentence before he was released.

This chapter of my life left open wounds so deep that only God could stitch me back together, and I hadn't met Him yet. He was there the whole time. I just didn't know how to reach out and take hold.

Sidenote: Much later in life, I came across a helpful handout from A Safe Place Ministries, and I have listed here a few notes from that handout:

In a brief moment, someone who chose to indulge his sinful passion for power and control chose you. Your life will never be the same again. You cannot undo the reality of the assault or the aftereffects that continue to shake your sense of safety and security. But hope and healing are possible. It will involve a commitment to move out of denial and a willingness to let others walk beside you through the valley of secrecy, guilt, shame, doubt, and fear, the valley that you now walk alone. Whether the assault happened yesterday or years ago, there is a way out of the pain. The effects of child sexual abuse are far-reaching—both in the present damage done to the developing child and in the child's future. The child must usually deal with the repercussions of the betrayal of trust, powerlessness, terror, and pain alone and in silence. "The average child makes nine attempts to disclose the abuse before someone responds. Boys often have more trouble than girls in saying they have been abused" (Doris Sandford, 1991). Adults abused as children often experience symptoms of post-traumatic stress disorder—intrusive memories, flashbacks, nightmares, dissociative episodes when present stressors trigger memories of the past trauma. Some common reactions to sexual assault include the following:

1. **Shock and disbelief:** Feeling numb and dazed, withdrawn and distant from other people. Desire to avoid people and places that remind you of the assault.

2. **Remembering what happened and what it felt like:** Unwanted memories, flashbacks, or nightmares. Reexperiencing some of the sensations and feelings you had during the assault, such as fear and powerlessness.

3. **Intense emotions:** Anger, anxiety, grief, depression.

4. **Physical symptoms:** Sleep disturbances, headaches, stomachaches, difficulty concentrating, and loss of interest in things formerly enjoyed.

5. **Fear.** Fear about personal safety, feeling powerless and vulnerable.

6. **Self-blame and shame.** Feeling dirty, devalued, humiliated, shameful or guilty.

Shock is the strongest emotion experienced by the victim. Shock leads to silence, a deafening silence that is not peaceful but paralyzing and debilitating. After a short period of time following the sexual abuse, anger toward the predator sets in. This anger can become compounded by the actions or inactions of one's parents. Even if positive action is immediately taken against the predator, the child victim of sexual abuse experiences irrational fear. The victims also experience the fear of failure that there was something they did or did not do that led to the sexual abuse. The end result of this fear is a deepening of the suffering silence that becomes a dark cloud always hovering over the victim, blocking any hope of relief. There is also a blending of "I did something bad" with "something bad happened to me." This blending becomes even stronger when parents or authorities refuse to take action against the predator. Guilt and shame can carry over into the long-term stage and factor into more complex and serious problems for the victim. Depression and isolation then take root. They are the offspring of guilt and shame. The longer no action is taken against the predator, the quicker depression and isolation come to the forefront. These psychological states affect the physical body. The psychological and the physical effects further deepen the suffering silence experienced by the child victim of sexual abuse. Isolation impacts the victim by creating the mindset of an intense loneliness that can be equated to being in a self-imposed quarantine. You believe you have this unexplainable disease that requires that you not be allowed to interact with anyone on a personal, intimate basis. Isolation sets you apart in such a way that you feel like an island away from contact with the mainland.

Shock, fear, guilt, shame, depression, and isolation create other characteristics manifested by the victim of child sexual abuse. The list of characteristics includes but is not limited to the following:

- Repeated nightmares and related sleep difficulties, including insomnia

- Eating disorders

- Secretiveness

- Unusual aggressive behavior without explanation or apparent cause

- Antisocial behavior

- School delinquency and truancy

- No interest in craft or other activities that require concentration (goes to depression)

- Intentionally breaking or destroying their personal possessions as well as those of others

- Alcohol/drug abuse

- Becoming sexually active early in life

- Suicidal thoughts

- Becoming prostitutes or child sexual abusers

In my life, I've experienced several of these characteristics. Some have been eliminated relatively easily, while others have taken much longer to overcome. There have been characteristics that I have not experienced, which goes to the fact that each victim reacts to child sexual abuse differently than others. There is no set pattern or formula that will accurately predict what a victim will do.

Thoughts for Survivors of Sexual Abuse

The assault was not your fault. The predator chose you because you were available. That also means that most likely, there was some degree of trust in place that the predator chose to betray.

You made the best choice that you could in the middle of the crisis, and you survived! Being abused did not fundamentally change your character, values, strengths, or positive attributes. It was a bad thing that happened *to* you, not *because of* you.

It is okay to ask for help. You may feel that if you avoid talking about the assault, you will be able to forget about what happened or keep the pain in tolerable proportions at the very least. Most survivors who try this approach eventually realize they need to talk to someone. If unresolved feelings and fears are holding you back from enjoying your life and participating fully in relationships, talking about the assault can help relieve some of the control it has over you and help you begin the process of recovery. A counselor who is trained to assist sexual assault victims will be able to understand the unique concerns you have and know ways to help you cope with the physical and emotional effects of the assault. A counselor can also help you deal with the reactions of family members and friends.

God is near to the brokenhearted and saves those crushed in spirit.
—Psalm 34:18

CHAPTER 2

EMOTIONAL SCARS

But the needy will not always be forgotten, nor the hope of the afflicted ever perish.

—Psalm 9:18

After we moved back to our hometown for my freshman year, I poured myself into sports. I drank when I could and bounced around relationships, wanting to fall in love so desperately, but because of the abuse, I was afraid to leave myself vulnerable. I tried to control everything in life, including sleeping with the first boy. When I met him at a rodeo dance and was severely inebriated, I decided to leave with him. We were kissing and groping when things progressed to a point that was out of control. Out of panic, I told him to stop, and he said he couldn't, so he didn't. Not only did I just suffer through my first sexual encounter, but he placed a huge hickey on my neck. I discovered the next day that he marked his conquests in this way so all the cowboys knew where he had been. I couldn't walk past people without the feeling that they were laughing, and I was filled with so much shame. I spent many years after this experience believing that when a boy/man started sex, he couldn't just stop without hurting himself, and that set me up for some nightmarish encounters. I wanted to fall in love but was afraid of the helplessness of being in a relationship. If I really cared for a boy, I would break up with him as soon as things started getting sexual and would end up having sex when I was drunk . . . with boys I had just met.

Aponi was my best friend and my baby sister, and so I devoted my time to hanging with her so that I could watch over her. One night after a party, I was driving home, and as I came around a corner, I hit black ice and went into a skid. I lay on the steering wheel, pulling hard right, and when we stopped, I found myself on the floorboards of the passenger side of the very large suburban. We climbed out and discovered somehow we had come to rest high up on a snowbank. Aponi started vomiting and blaming my driving, but she had drunk quite a bit. It was around two in the morning, so we started walking down the road to a house so we could use the phone to call our mom. Aponi was walking behind and griping about my driving when she stepped on the very same patch of black ice that had started the skid and fell on her backside. Faith's boyfriend came to our rescue and drove us home, and then the next day, friends had to get a tractor to pull the vehicle out. Everyone was amazed because there were no tracks leading up the snowbank and the suburban was sitting high. They all commented that it looked like we had flown and had been set down on top of the snowbank. I now believe God had been with me most of my life. I just never knew Him at that point. Why would He love me? But He did and would never give up on me.

Our mom married during my junior year of high school, and I just adored my new stepdad. He would cook breakfast and do silly things to make me laugh, but problems soon started with him and Mom. He brought her home from the bar one night, and she wanted to go back; however, he refused to let her go, so she caught her horse and proceeded to ride the twelve miles to town. The next thing we knew, the phone was ringing to tell us that she was at the ER. She had fallen off her horse and hit her head on a rock.

Our mother's marriage only lasted a year, and so we moved into town the beginning of my senior year of high school. I brought in the Fourth of July by being passed out by noon and back to drinking by 2:00 p.m. Though I used alcohol to cope with life, I also loved my sports and poured myself into being the best I could. I had spent my sixteenth birthday the year before drinking a bottle of peppermint Schnapps and attending the *Rocky Horror Picture Show,* of which I spent most the time passed out in the bathroom. Aponi had to get some guys to help get me out without anyone noticing I was wasted. A few months later, I called the US Air Force recruiter and decided to join and leave as soon as I graduated the following year.

One night, I was out with a boy and got really drunk, and between blackouts, I could kind of remember being out on a secluded road and him racing back to town and driving Sunny's car. He drove me to the restaurant and went inside, leaving me semiconscious in the car. My ex "boyfriend" had words with him and then put me in his car and drove home, carrying me to my bedroom and placing me tenderly in bed. I believe I was raped that night out in that secluded area. If I was, nothing was ever said, and I was so drunk I couldn't remember. My mom came into the bedroom much later, demanding to know where my sister's car was, and I couldn't tell her because I honestly had no idea. I didn't think I had drunk that much and felt that maybe I had been drugged and the need to escape this town was overwhelming. So between basketball games and cheering, I did all the in-processing, tests, and physicals required for the US Air Force.

With about three months left of school, Mom decided she was taking the other kids and leaving. I was moved into the attic of one of her friend's home so that I could finish out high school, and they moved to a town about an hour away. I ran the hurdles at state on May 21 and then got home in time to change for my graduation ceremony. Exactly one month later at seventeen years of age, I was on the plane to basic training in San Antonio, Texas

I had never been on a plane until the day I flew out of Idaho headed for San Antonio and the US Air Force. I kept telling myself that life was an adventure and I was just off on one of many experiences yet to come. I was running hard away from the life I had had and hoped for a future full of joy, love, and laughter—a new beginning. As I stepped off the plane, I felt as if someone had thrown a bucket of water at my face. The air was so humid compared to Idaho, but I survived the six weeks of basic very easily—except for a few minor mishaps, one being the first morning when my TI (training instructor) came in. I smiled at him. I had only seen a few black men in my life, and this man was a huge one. He got in my face and asked if he looked funny to me. He said that I needed to wipe that smile off my face. I had learned to always smile when I was scared or upset, so it took everything I had to not smile—a very hard lesson to learn. Then when we went down to eat and I had finished, I crossed what is known as the snake pit and went out the door only to realize I was on the wrong side of the building, the men's side. They were all in formation and staring at me. I turned around, but the door had already closed and locked. Thankfully, another TI had followed me and quickly told me to get back on the other side as he held the door open.

At one point, my hair got too long, and so they sent me to the base barber for a haircut. When the barber spun me back around to the mirror, I wanted to cry at the reflection staring back. My hair was really short, and my Dumbo-sized ears were poking out. When I got back to the barracks, the others said I looked like Howdy Doody and were all laughing and cracking jokes. Thankfully at that time, I had no clue about who Howdy Doody was.

After I graduated basic, I was loaded on a bus and sent to Shepard AFB at Wichita Falls, Texas, for tech school. I was going to train to work the air passenger service. Even though I was only seventeen, I was able to drink at the club on base, and I loved to go dancing.

I soon fell head over heels for a guy, I will call him G, and spent any spare time with him. We would sit outside and talk until curfew or go to the movies or dancing. I had grown up with a very racial father, and G was black, so I knew my father would not approve. G waited until I was eighteen, and then we spent the night together off base at a hotel. He became the first guy I was with during which I was not drunk, but a few days after this magical night, we had to go on leave back to our hometowns. Then he was sent to Korea, and I received orders for the Philippines. He went on to Korea, and two weeks after I turned eighteen, I was on a plane headed for Manila in the Philippines.

By changing my life, I had shoved the wounds down deep, and I hoped to never have to deal with them again. I didn't realize that wounds left untreated fester and infect the whole body before they turn to scars.

CHAPTER 3

A NEW BEGINNING

There is a way that seems right to a man, but its end is the way of death.

—Proverbs 14:12 NIV

On the eighteen-hour or so flight to Manila, I met a man who was in the US Navy. He was stationed in the Philippines and headed back from the States. He said that his wife was meeting him at the airport but that he would help me get through customs and directed to the US Air Force bus. Upon arrival, the passengers were hustled through customs, and then he pointed out the bus. As I stepped outside, I was swarmed with children wanting to help with the luggage. They didn't give me a chance to say no and carried it all on the bus. I thought about what sweet kids they were. Then they turned around and held their hands out for pesos. Coming from rural Idaho, I didn't have a clue what a peso was, but thankfully, someone on the bus paid the children for me and then explained. On the bus trip to Clark AB, the other passengers told me stories of what to expect, ranging from cobras crawling around to lizards called geckos that crawled all over your bedroom walls. I later would learn that off base was "bar row" with over five hundred bars stretching along the perimeter, and in each bar were "hostesses," young local girls dancing in bathing suits on stage and putting on shows to be purchased for two hundred pesos ($10.00) for the night.

I arrived late, and so was placed in a dorm room for the night and informed that someone would be by to get me in the morning. I turned off the light and tumbled wearily into bed only to hear a chirping sound. I got up and turned the light on to discover a gecko crawling along the wall. I spent the remainder of the night with the light on and very little sleep.

After in-processing I discovered the base had a women's basketball team, and I joined. I kept busy with work, ball, and partying with newfound friends. G and I wrote constantly, and I remained loyal to him. The ball team got to travel to other countries for tournaments, and I got to see Korea, Okinawa, and Yokota AB, Japan. Some of the women on my team were officers who had played college ball or from much larger schools. I became an asset only because I was fast and could get in front of the other teams ball handlers and take the hit for them to foul out. The coaches would match me up and tell me to get them to foul out. We played with international rules, which were all foreign to me, and we played the local colleges, so we spent a few games getting pinched and bruised by the girls from the college in Manila.

The following summer, I flew to Korea to see G for my vacation rather than going back to the States for family. I wanted so desperately to be married and start a family, but my week there made me feel that he was embarrassed of me and hid me out at the hotel. I left there realizing his plans and mine were not lining up, and I didn't think he cared for me the way I did for him. By the time my birthday arrived two months later, I was sure our relationship was on a one-way track because I hadn't received any acknowledgment from him that he even remembered my birthday. In the back of my mind, I kept hearing Mom tell me that if I could not bring my babies home, I should not be in a relationship with that person. My dad was so racial along with the area I grew up in, Idaho. My babies would have suffered. So out of loneliness, I started looking for someone else. Because of the STDs that seem to run rampant, I wanted a man who had just came from the

States. I was very uneducated about how condoms protected against STDs and was only focused on birth control. The men just laughed about the STDs and the long lines at the clinic on Mondays reaching clear down the hall for their shots. They called it "the Drip."

On my birthday, a guy, Dick, who would be working with the cargo side of our group, arrived and he would be a roommate to one of the guys in our little group of friends. After I slept with Dick, I received a gift in the mail from G for my birthday, but it was too late. One day as I was headed to work and stepped out the door, I saw Dick sitting on the steps of his dorm just across the yard and waiting for me. He told me he needed to talk. It seems that after he was telling me good night, he was going out with other ladies and ended up with an STD. I needed to go to the doctor for a shot. Left hurt and speechless, I went through the humiliation of telling the clinic why I was there and suffered through the shot, which had to be given in the backside. Then I forgave Dick and continued dating him until a few weeks later, I stepped out the door and again found him sitting there. My heart just sank at this sight, knowing what he was going to say. It seems he was going from my room to a few other ladies in my own dorm, ones I faced on a daily basis, and I had no idea. Numbly, I went and got another shot and told him to stay away. A few days later, I was out with the friends, and one of the "hostesses" was asking where Dick was, so I asked her how she knew him. The girl told me how Dick was going to marry her and how she loved him and had been dating him for some time. The worst part was that he was part of my circle of friends, so I had to endure him being around.

Being away from home for Christmas is probably one of the hardest parts of military life. I bought a fake tree and decorations, and my friends and I decorated my room and then had a toga party. D, another guy who was part of the group and had become a good friend, had always flirted with me, but being lonely on this night and the drinking made us a little careless. He kissed me, and one thing led to another until we found ourselves in bed. When we were not working, we spent all our time together, and then one evening after drinking and dancing, I just broke down and started bawling about Uncle Alvah and the abuse. D just held me while I had a breakdown and sobbed until I fell asleep in his arms. I awoke the next morning with him sitting in a chair next to the bed, just staring at me with a loving smile. He pushed my hair back from my face and kissed me affectionately on the forehead and then told me to forgive myself because none of the abuse to me or my sisters had been my fault. A small part of me knew he was right and would start to heal just a little. No one had ever told me that I was not to blame, and so I had carried that festering guilt in my heart all those years, thinking I was not good enough or I had done something to deserve that kind of treatment. Shortly after that, D headed back to the States on vacation. While he was gone, things got really uncomfortable around our group of friends until finally someone decided I should know that D had gone back to the States to get married. Turns out he had had a fiancé the whole time I had been with him.

I was barely nineteen years old and found myself battling alcoholism. I was working all day, going home, and fixing a drink while I showered and got ready. I went to dinner with a drink and then head off base to drink the night away and then stumbled home only to get up and do it all over again. Loneliness got so fierce at times I would cling to anything or anybody to keep it at bay. I was starving for love and affection but terrified of it at the same time. To quit drinking so much and fill my time more productively, I started taking college classes, and Don, a guy from one of the other dorms, would give me rides every now and then. We had nothing in common, although I thought he was cute.

All of my friends got orders, and one by one, they shipped out, mostly going to Spain. I was the only one with orders to Yokota AB, Japan. During the out-processing, my office held a going-away party, and we were all to meet up and go dancing. I only met up with a few, and the next morning, there was a knock at my door. My supervisor was there to say that Nanette, one of the sweetest girls we worked with, had died the night before. Instead of going dancing, she had gone home, and she was awoken up by a cobra in her living room. The property owners had burned the fields that day around her house, and the snakes had moved to cover. She was bitten, and she ran to her sister's room to get help. They tried to get her on base; however, she needed her uncle to get the pass, and no one could find him in time. She succumbed to the cobra's poison before anyone could help her. I was devastated at the news and went out to drink my sorrows away that evening. I left Clark AB wanting nothing to do with men but wanting a family terribly. I had a deep ache to be loved, always that desperate driving force to just have someone love me.

CHAPTER 4

NIGHTMARES

He reached down from on high and took hold of me; he drew me out of
the deep waters.

—Psalm 18:16

After two weeks of leave with family in Idaho, I headed to Japan at nineteen years of age. After I arrived and the staff started in-processing to the base, I bought my first car off the lemon lot. Japanese drive on the opposite side of the road, so the car had the steering wheel on the right-hand side, and I had to learn to shift using my left hand. I wandered off base within the first week and got lost, but before panic set in very much, I was able to follow the fence around the base until I arrived at a gate to get back on. My explorations were on foot or train after that.

Within the first few days, I ran into a familiar face from Clark AB, and he said he was going to a birthday party and wanted to know if I wanted to go along. We went to the birthday party, and it turned out the party was for Don, the guy I had taken classes with at Clark AB and ridden back and forth from the dorms with. Within a few weeks, we were dating, and before long, I fancied myself in love with him. We spent some of the weekends camping with the Japanese locals down by the river. He was six years older than me and would be separating from the service by the end of the year.

After we had been dating for about four months, he took me to dinner, and right in the middle of a crowded restaurant, he informed me he was married. He had a story about getting a girl back home pregnant and how he had to marry her, and then she had lost the baby, so he was just getting ready to do the divorce procedures. I was speechless but supportive. Two days later, he told me he had lied and that he had actually married his stepmom's younger sister to help her get her green card and that one of the "cousins" who had flown out to see him a month earlier had actually been his wife. I wanted so desperately to be a loving wife and be a stay-at-home mom to take care of all the children I was going to have, with a loving husband who worked to provide for us. Having a baby meant the world to me.

That November, Don separated from the US Air Force and left me distraught at the terminal gate. He was headed to California for a brief vacation before he headed to Hawaii to live and go to school, and I was going to fly out in June, the month when we would get married. That weekend, I started vomiting and couldn't get out of bed. I thought I had food poisoning from the pizza, so I went to the doctor the following Monday, and he asked me if I could be pregnant. I was told to come back in a week for another test. Don had only been gone less than two weeks when I discovered I was pregnant. Twenty years old, living in another country all alone, and I was pregnant. You would think I would have fallen apart, but it was the greatest news of my life. I was finally going to get my family and have all the unconditional love I could ever dream of. I would not have to try to earn love anymore.

As it got closer to the holidays, Don called and begged for me to fly to Hawaii for New Year's. Everyone expected me to come back married, myself included. So I loaded onto an airplane and headed to Hawaii. Except for major morning sickness, we had an amazing time, and Don did propose. We spent New Year's Eve on the beach, watching fireworks. He took me to North Shore, and we ate strawberries on the beach and then went to a bungalow on the beach. And that is where things went horribly wrong. I realized he was still married. He had not filed for divorce like he said he was going to. He told me he was going to stay married until May. And then we would get married in June, and our baby would arrive in July. He told me how I would reenlist and support him while he went to college and cared for our baby, and then he continued on with how our child would attend a private school. I loaned him money to get registered for college, and while he drove into town to register, I had time to think and came to realize I had no say in my future if I stayed with this man. He didn't once ask what I wanted and made plans for my whole life. Plus, the fact he hadn't gotten divorced made me believe the baby and I were not priorities on his list, and I so desperately needed to be first on someone's list. By the time he got back, I told him I was breaking up and walking away. He threatened to take the baby and then told me that if it was a girl, I could have her. I would get a boy until he was five, and then Don got him. And twins would be split.

I left Hawaii, knowing he would not be a part of my baby's life. I was pregnant, single, and living in another country, but I had no doubt I could do it. Nothing would steal my joy of being a mom, but shortly after I got back to Japan, the dreams started. I would wake up trembling from nightmares that Don had taken my baby and disappeared. It was the same dream over and over. We were at a playground. I would turn around for something, and when I turned back, my baby was gone. I would wake up crying uncontrollably and drenched in sweat and knew I had to protect my baby at all costs. Then the nightmares slowly faded to a beautiful dream. One night, I had another dream. I was talking to my grandmother, who had passed when I was twelve. I dreamed she was sitting at her sewing machine and I was kneeling by her side. She brushed the tears away and told me everything was going to be all right. I then woke up feeling at peace with what was going on in my life. Once I moved off base to my apartment, I started having dreams of Jesus sitting in this huge rocking chair, bending over, and lifting me out of bed and onto His lap, where He would hold me and rock me to sleep. It was such a powerful dream that gave me so much peace. I knew I could get through whatever was coming my way. Going from not believing I was good enough for God to have Jesus rock me to sleep shows the journey my faith was beginning to take, but it would still be years before I would fully understand the depth of the Lord's love and forgiveness.

A few weeks before the due date, my doctor told me I was close and needed to stay on base all weekend. I told him I lived off base, so he told me not to be alone. I told him I lived by myself. I worked all day that Saturday at the dispatch station, but I was having contractions on and off, some being pretty intense. My shift was from 5:00 a.m. to 1:00 p.m., and when I got off, I headed home to take a nap and lie on a heating pad. I awoke some time later and ate a peanut butter sandwich and drank a glass of milk before I realized the contractions were less than five minutes apart and had a definite pattern to them. I started panicking and hurriedly got my stuff together and headed for the base. I had to drive through Japanese traffic with major contractions and a stick shift. It was not a fun situation, and I was trying to breathe and to keep from hyperventilating and letting fear overtake me. I finally arrived at the air terminal to pick up Merry, my previous roommate and dear friend, only to discover she was out on the flight line. The crew sent another bus out to relieve her while another co-worker walked with me and helped me to breathe. I kept almost hyperventilating, and fear was starting to take over by the time Merry hurried in and we headed to the hospital.

They wheeled me into the sterile delivery room while Merry got dressed in sterile clothing and had me crawl from one bed to another. The doctor arrived just as I was able to push, and my baby boy was born. There is no greater joy in this world than giving birth and being able to hold your baby for the first time. Words could not describe the feelings I experienced. The fierce emotions of love and protectiveness, no one was ever going to hurt my baby the way I had been hurt. I was so worried from the dreams of Don taking him that I left his name off the birth certificate. John was my baby, and no one was going to ever hurt him.

The love I felt for this little guy is what I had been searching for, and he became the center of my universe. I had to go back to work when he was four weeks old and found a military dependent to babysit. I was getting up at 3:00 a.m. to get ready for work, drop him off, and work from five to one. Then we would go home and snuggle for nap time. About two weeks after I returned to work, I discovered a guy had been asking about me and wanted to date. He knew all about my situation and didn't mind. I had lunch with Dwayne, and we hit it off really well. He told me how his mom was Japanese and his dad had served for the state police and lost his legs in an accident. Then after we dated a few months, he told me how his ex-girlfriend had a baby girl and his mom said she had his eyes, so he thought he had a baby. He even said her name was Rene Lynn, which was the name he and his ex-girlfriend had wanted to name their baby girl. I supported him in all he told me, not thinking for once he was lying. After all, what reason would he have for making up all this?

We talked about marriage and how I would get out of the service. He said he would reenlist to take care of us. This was my dream after all, so it sounded great.

Sometimes you can be afflicted with small continuous wounds and not realize they are painful until many years later.

CHAPTER 5

BETRAYALS

Remember not the sins of my youth and my rebellious ways according to
your love remember me, for you are good, O Lord.

—Psalm 25:7

I left Japan with a nine-month-old to fly to California and catch a bus to the Air Force base to separate from the service. I was overwhelmed with all I needed for the trip from the car seat, suitcases, formula, and baby food that John would need for the next few days. I then flew home with my baby to meet his grandparents. I was at a loss trying to figure out what to do with my life. When Dwayne got to Ohio, we talked. I truly missed him, so John and I flew there. I was completely and utterly dumbfounded when Dwayne and his father came strolling up to greet me at the airport and discover that his mom was not Japanese. I never brought it up to him, but when I asked his sister if Dwayne's ex had a baby girl, I was informed there was a baby but it was a boy. I was really confused about what to do at this point. I was single with a baby and no job. The man I thought I had fallen in love with hadn't told me a single truth about his life. I was getting ready to fly back to Idaho, and then he asked me to marry him and follow him to Louisiana, so I did. We were married at the courthouse with just his family and none of mine, and then I waited with his parents in Ohio while he was processed at his base and he sent for us.

He already had an apartment when I got there, and he had bought a station wagon. The stay-at-home mom I had dreamed of being wasn't going so well. I felt so alone, and we didn't have any money to do anything. He wouldn't take me anywhere on base, and he kept me isolated from his friends. I decided to get a job, and I actually got an interview with an airline to work at their counter doing what I had done in the US Air Force. After I drove to Houston for an interview and was selected as a potential candidate, they informed me that I would have to commute daily to another airport, so I had to decline. Shortly afterward, I discovered I was pregnant. I was so excited but worried at the same time about finances, so I took a job at Burger King, where I worked throughout the pregnancy.

Dwayne promised me he had no contact with his ex, and I finally confronted him about all the stories he had given about his parents and supposedly having a child. He asked that I never bring it up again but gave no excuse as to why he would tell me something like that.

My second child, Broc, was so fussy that I stressed constantly. He wouldn't snuggle, and he seemed to cry continuously. I would take him to the ER, and the nurses would tell me I was just an overstressed young mother. To add to that stress, I discovered I needed surgery to have all four of my wisdom teeth pulled. Dwayne drove me to and from the appointment. I was gassed and didn't wake up until that evening. He was jostling me awake to inform me he was going fishing that night and I needed to get up and take care of the boys. I later discovered just how great of a caretaker he was, and I say this with great sarcasm. He had left me in the car while going into the video store to rent movies and then drove through the Burger King drive-through, where my co-workers and he had a good laugh over me. And worse, he drove out to the lake and went fishing while he left me in the car. I don't know how long after surgery he waited before he finally took me home and placed me on our bed only to wake me up later so he could go fishing.

My days consisted of getting up at 3:00 a.m., running his bathwater, laying out his clothes, getting him up, and then loading the kids into the car to take him to work. I would spend the day cleaning and preparing their dinner so that Dwayne would not have to cook. I would then pick him up from work and drop them off at the house and rush off to work till 11:00 p.m. I would go home and iron his uniforms and unwind and crawl into bed by midnight only to get up and do it again. My health started to deteriorate at this point, and I was put on some kind of nerve pills and muscle relaxers.

I had a feeling he was still in contact with his ex-girlfriend, so I called the navy base where she was stationed for information to get her work number, and then I called her. She was out of the office, but her husband answered the phone. Things couldn't have been planned any better because ten minutes after I asked him if he knew my husband and he said no and I told him how his wife did and she needed to leave us alone, Dwayne showed up in the driveway. He flew out of the car and came crashing furiously into the house. He got in my face, demanding to know why I would call his ex's husband. I just looked at him with a calm face and said, "For not having any contact with her, she sure knew what number to call to complain." And the look on his face as he realized he was caught in another lie was all the confirmation I needed.

Dwayne got orders to Korea shortly afterward but refused to let me move to Idaho, where my family lived. I had to move to Ohio and live with his parents for the year he would be gone. I then drove to Ohio with my two babies, John not quite three and Broc barely over one. Dwayne flew in and spent a few weeks with us and then left for Korea.

I got a job and spent the days playing with the boys and working swing shifts while Dwayne's parents babysat. Dwayne would call when he could, and on one such call as we were talking, he said, "Hey, Jules." When I asked who that was, he said it was a girl in his dorm who had just walked past. My friend Merry, who had helped deliver John and had been my roommate in Japan, wrote to tell me she was in Korea and had seen Dwayne hanging with this girl named Juliet. Dwayne, of course, denied it and told me Merry was just jealous and trying to make problems and that she had asked to spend the night with him and he had turned her down. I believed him and threw away a wonderful friendship.

My gut feeling was that Merry was telling the truth, so I decided it was time to go back to Idaho. I loaded up my two boys and drove across the country with them. It took three days, and I had plenty of time to think about my marriage. I was willing to hang on till he got back from Korea. I asked him to come home at his six-month mark, but he didn't seem interested in saving our marriage and said he was not coming to Idaho. In January, I filed for divorce, and it seemed my intuition was right because we were divorced in April. That was the same month Dwayne and Juliet or "Jules" were married.

I had driven with my family to Aponi's wedding in California and ran into Allen, my first love from fifth grade. We had even walked together at high school graduation. After the divorce was final, I packed up and moved my boys to California. Then Allen and I were married in June. I had been so in love with the guy I knew from high school that I didn't take the time to get to know him now. I became pregnant shortly after our wedding and worked up until I was six months along. I started having complications and could not work any longer. Things were going wrong at home with Allen and the boys. He did have not the patience he had started with, and one time, he spanked Broc for something minor. By the time I got into the room, Broc had a bloody nose. I told Allen to get out of the house. In between comforting my son and tears, Allen begged to stay and promised to never lay another hand on them, and I believed him.

April brought a daughter we named Daisy into our lives, and life seemed so tranquil that I felt for the first time things were going to be all right. That feeling lasted only the six weeks I was home before I had to go back to work. Two weeks into going back to work, I was so stressed and exhausted that my milk supply dried up, and Allen was not handling the night feeding well.

Allen used the boys as a stress relief by scolding them constantly, and now that he couldn't spank them, he resorted to putting them in corners for hours on end and forgetting about them. We fought about discipline constantly, and I started hating the situation as old feelings of fleeing kept creeping in, but I had just had my third child from the third different man and knew I could not run anymore. One weekend, Aponi and I decided to go out, so I arranged for a babysitter so that Allen could go with us because he had never taken me out. He decided he didn't want to go at the last moment and said I couldn't either, which only made me want to go even more. We fought about it the whole time I got ready, and then Aponi arrived. Turns out leaving the house when you're severely angry at your husband, feeling lost and alone in your marriage with a husband that is physically abusive to your kids is not a good combination, and old habits won out. I drank way too much and ended up sleeping with a complete stranger and then denied it for years. I thought that if I admitted it to Allen, it would prove what kind of horrible person I was. I felt filthy and more alone than ever, and with all those times of being lied to and cheated on, now I was just like those men. I made the decision that if Allen would stay with me, I would do whatever it took to save our marriage.

I felt so trapped and actually started trying to pray, but after what I did, I knew God would not answer. One day when things seemed the lowest, the doorbell rang, and Jehovah Witnesses were there. We started talking, and I felt this tremendous thirst for more of God's Word. In time, we started doing in-home Bible studies. At first, it felt right, but then some of the answers they gave didn't seem to give me peace. I started praying every night at bedtime, and we fell into a routine of me raising the kids while Allen worked all day and watched TV all night. I found joy in my children, although Broc made me cry more than the other children. He also made me laugh more. One time when Daisy was a baby, we went to the store, and I told Broc to stand beside the truck while I put Daisy in the car seat. I turned my back for only a minute, but when I turned back around, Broc was still standing in the same place, except now he had a perfect black circle around his eye. I just stood there dumbfounded, trying to figure out what he had done, and then it dawned on me that while my back was turned, his little inquisitive nature led him to grab ahold of the tailpipe and place his eye on it to see inside.

John was in first grade when he came home one day upset because he wanted to know who is father was. I tracked Don down, and we made arrangements for John to fly escorted to see his dad for the first time. He was a month from his sixth birthday, and as hard as it was because of the dreams, I placed him on the plane. Don called when John was due to fly in and acted like he couldn't find him. I was so upset, and he just laughed.

In 1993, Allen's dad had a heart attack, so we decided to move back to Idaho to be closer to family and let our kids know their grandparents. We settled in, and I started looking for work. After a few months, I got a job as an operator at a major semiconductor company in Boise. Allen slowly started to get his self-employed contractor business up and running. I worked three days on one week and four the other so our kids had to go to a daycare. Our life was running smoothly, and we had insurance for the first time since I had quit work when Daisy was a baby. I started taking college classes so I could get promoted. I loved my job. The people I worked with became like a second family.

All my dreams had come true. I just had to keep that one night of betrayal hidden deep for no one except my baby sis to ever know. The trouble is that sins like these fester ooze and they are always present subconsciously. The nightmare of my childhood and Uncle Alvah was always present, for even my husband could not wake me up in the middle of the night without bringing on anxiety attacks. The end of 1994, I discovered I was pregnant and was so excited because I would have a baby born in Idaho and around family, so they could be a part of watching him or her grow from the first day on.

CHAPTER 6

THE WRATH OF GOD

You will keep in perfect peace him whose mind is steadfast, because he trusts in you.

—Isaiah 26:3

My doctor appointments started off normal enough, but at the twelve-week checkup when the doctor couldn't hear the heartbeat, she was slightly concerned and asked that I return in two weeks instead of four. I was stressed because with my other three pregnancies, I had been able to hear the heartbeat by ten weeks. At fourteen weeks, there was still no heartbeat, and yet the doctor wished to wait another two weeks. Just shy of sixteen weeks, I went back, and when the doctor still couldn't hear the beat, she scheduled me for an ultrasound. I drove to Allen's worksite and picked him up, and we dropped the kids off with a babysitter as we headed out of town. I felt like something was horribly wrong. While I was lying on the table, the technician turned on the equipment, and my fears was instantly realized. Our baby was motionless and just floated around in my womb with no sign of life. I had ultrasounds with the other pregnancies and knew my baby should be bouncing with a recognizable heartbeat. I kept asking the technicians if everything was all right, and while she was avoiding all eye contact, she said her office would send the results over to another doctor's office and that we needed to go directly to her office from there.

I cried all the way back to the doctor's office. The ultrasound showed the baby had died at thirteen weeks but my body was not aborting, which could cause serious toxic health problems, so I was scheduled for a dilatation and curettage the next day. I came out of the surgery with the understanding that the placenta was too attached to separate, so I was supposed to take some pills to cause my body to abort the fetus, and then I was sent home with instructions to bring any large pieces of tissue in for evaluation to see what caused the baby to die. I went home, still numb from losing my baby, and woke up the next day, severely cramping. By afternoon, I was literally on the living room floor on my hands and knees, thinking it felt a lot like labor but couldn't comprehend why. I went to the restroom, and something dropped. When I reached for it, I had to give it a tug, and when I pulled up, I was holding my baby in the palm of my hand. The baby's little arm flopped lifelessly to the side, and everything just faded away briefly. I was gasping for air and trying to maintain some form of control as I folded my baby in some tissue and placed her in a cup. I had to keep my composure because I was home alone with my four-year-old daughter. I needed to get to the school to gather up the boys and drive to the clinic. One look at me, and the staff rushed me out of the waiting area and into a waiting room. The doctor took my baby and opened up the tissue. Her comment was this: "Yes, this is the fetus." I lost all sense of reality at that point and yelled at her that it was my baby, which I had thought she had removed during the procedure. The doctor remained calm and asked if the placenta had detached yet, and because it had not, she sent me home. She said that if it did not detach within another day, I would have to have surgery again.

Unable to breathe and feeling like I was slowly drowning, I rushed out, leaving my baby with the clinic, and drove home in a fog to crawl into bed. I called Allen and begged him to get home, using the excuse the kids were out of control and I couldn't handle them. As soon as he arrived, I started bawling hysterically while he held me and I explained what had happened. The next few weeks, I went through the motions of mourning and dealing with the guilt, believing it was my fault for cheating on Allen. God was punishing me for my sin. I knew I deserved what was happening; however, my family did not, and it became just another wound that would be a scar on my heart, one pushed down but not forgotten. It was probably the closest I had ever come to feeling like I was losing my mind and going over the edge with no way of returning.

I then poured myself into classes even more, and when a promotion opportunity came, I was ready to apply and got accepted as a technician. We bought a house, and I started to realize that when something bad happened, something good would also happen. It became my roller-coaster ride. When I hit bottom, I would look for the good, and soon, it would appear. That fall, I discovered I was pregnant again. I was so thankful but also guarded until I was able to hear the strong heartbeat of my baby. Although I had been vaccinated when I had gone overseas for the US Air Force, the doctor noted I was susceptible to catching the measles. For some reason, my immune system had changed.

With my new job, I had to pull rotations and had to work three months of graveyard shifts. I loved my new job, and the people I worked with became my little family away from home. About halfway through my pregnancy, I started having pain in my upper right side, but the doctors insisted the baby was just pushing up on my organs. Allen called one day while I was home sleeping after I had worked a night shift and said he had fallen off a roof and broken his hand and was headed to the doctor. Sure enough, he came home with a cast and pain pills, and our life would never be the same. I became aware a few months later that we were dealing with drug abuse of prescription pain meds because he was going to the doctor regularly for refills even after the pain should have been gone.

On August 25 after a restless night, I decided to go into work early. Being back on the day shift that Sunday, I drove the hour to work, but I was having cramps and just not feeling well. After I drank a 7UP to settle my stomach, I started vomiting. I called the nurse, who told me to come in and be checked. It was still two weeks before my due date. I got to the hospital, and the nurses ran some blood work and came in to inform me that I should call my husband because I was being admitted and needed to have the baby delivered by the end of the day. Turns out my liver enzymes, alkaline phosphates, were extremely high. Actually extremely, high would be an understatement. I called Allen, and he hurried over as I was transferred to a labor/delivery room and given the Pitocin gel to start labor progressing. My nurse ran the water for the jet tub and never checked it before I went to climb in, and I scalded myself. Finally, our little guy, Cody, made his entrance that evening, but his body temperature was so low, the nurse took him immediately with Allen to try to get warmed up in the nursery.

The doctor kept me for two extra days in the hospital to run tests to find out why my enzymes were so out of control. He mentioned things, such as lupus, cancer, and so on, or he said it could just be pregnancy-related, so I had ultrasounds and blood work done during those two days. After he released me, he monitored me closely for three months and then decided it was not pregnancy-related and I needed to see a specialist. So he sent me to a gastroenterologist. He ran blood work for six more months, ruling out everything he could possibly think of. At one time, they drew nine vials of blood in one sitting. I went back to work after Cody was three months old, and after six more months of tests and still nothing, it was time to start doing invasive tests.

The first medical test was when Cody was nine months old—a colonoscopy. And to prep, I had to down a cleansing drink a few days prior, one that would not have been so bad had I not been nursing at the time. I was literally running for the bathroom while I was drinking the cleanser. I would try to nurse and then throw him on the couch, yell at someone to watch him, and run for the bathroom. The result from that test came back that I had ulcerative colitis, and the doctor said 70 percent of people with this and my enzyme counts usually have a rare liver disease. So then I was scheduled for an ERCP, which is a procedure when the scope is guided down the throat, and again, results pointed toward the liver, so then I had to have a liver biopsy.

Allen wasn't working much, so he took care of Cody, and if he did have a job, he would take Cody along with him so that we would not have to leave Cody in a daycare. The liver biopsy came back positive for primary sclerosing cholangitis in the earliest of stages. At the same time, Walter Payton, a former pro football player, was also diagnosed, and as I watched the media show his decline, I feared for my own life. The doctor said the given life span if left untreated was about twelve years.

I went into a state of depression and figured if I wasn't going to see my kids grow up, I may as well back out then and let them learn to live without me. There is no way to explain my reasoning. It was just how I dealt with the news. So I buried myself in the job and college classes even more only to wake up one day with the realization that the man I was married to had an addiction to pain pills that was completely out of control. At this time, I also decided that if I was going to die, I needed to give the kids as many memories as I could, so I started spending as much time with them as possible to make as many happy memories as possible. I coached their sports and volunteered as art mom at the school, even though I had no artistic talent whatsoever. I stressed quality more than quantity in this time together, but in time, I would realize that quantity is just as important to a child. They need their parents in their lives.

Miscarriage

This is only my opinion. I believe that a baby is alive at the moment of conception, and so when the doctor was talking about tissue, I was misunderstanding what she meant. The loss of a baby at any stage of pregnancy should be mourned as a loss of a child, and thankfully, I had many friends and co-workers who understood this and sent me flowers and sympathy cards for our family's loss. I took my loss extra hard because of the guilt I was carrying over my sin. The lesson I learned since then is that God does not test us but allows us to be tested and does not give us more than we can handle. This was a process over many years before I was given relief of my guilt. I was able to have a perfectly healthy baby within a year of this miscarriage.

Ulcerative Colitis

Ulcerative colitis is an inflammatory bowel disease (IBD) that causes long-lasting inflammation in part of your digestive tract.

Ulcerative colitis can be debilitating and sometimes can lead to life-threatening complications. Because ulcerative colitis is a chronic condition, symptoms usually develop over time rather than suddenly.

Ulcerative colitis usually affects only the innermost lining of your large intestine (colon) and rectum. It occurs only through continuous stretches of your colon, unlike Crohn's disease, which occurs anywhere in the digestive tract and often spreads deeply into the affected tissues.

There's no known cure for ulcerative colitis, but therapies are available that may dramatically reduce the signs and symptoms of ulcerative colitis and even bring about a long-term remission.

Although ulcerative colitis usually isn't fatal, it's a serious disease that may cause life-threatening complications in some cases.

Like Crohn's disease, ulcerative colitis causes inflammation and ulcers in your intestine. But unlike Crohn's, which can affect the colon in various separate sections, ulcerative colitis usually affects one continuous section of the inner lining of the colon beginning with the rectum.

No one is quite sure what triggers ulcerative colitis, but there's a consensus as to what doesn't. Researchers no longer believe that stress is the main cause, although stress can often aggravate symptoms.

Sometimes you may feel helpless when you are facing ulcerative colitis. But changes in your diet and lifestyle may help control your symptoms and lengthen the time between flare-ups.

Primary Sclerosing Cholangitis

Primary sclerosing cholangitis is a disease of the bile ducts in your liver. The term "cholangitis" in primary sclerosing cholangitis refers to inflammation of the bile ducts, while the term "sclerosing" describes the hardening and scarring of the bile ducts that result from chronic inflammation.

Primary sclerosing cholangitis is a progressive disease that eventually leads to liver damage and liver failure. Liver transplant is the only known cure for primary sclerosing cholangitis, but transplants are typically reserved for people with severe liver damage.

Researchers continue looking for treatments to slow or reverse bile duct damage caused by primary sclerosing cholangitis. But until a treatment is found, doctors care for people with primary sclerosing cholangitis by reducing signs and symptoms of complications.

Primary sclerosing cholangitis may not cause any symptoms in its early stages. In some cases, the only indication of this disorder may be abnormal blood tests suggesting that your liver isn't functioning well.

It's not clear what causes primary sclerosing cholangitis. Many believe that the condition may be caused by an immune system reaction to an infection or toxin in people with a predisposition to develop the disease.

Primary sclerosing cholangitis occurs more frequently in people with other medical conditions, particularly inflammatory bowel disease. It's not clear how these conditions are linked and if they share similar causes.

CHAPTER 7

CANCER

AT DAY'S END: *Is anybody happier because you passed his way? Does anyone remember that you spoke to him today? The day is almost over, and its toiling time is through. Is there anyone to utter now a kindly word of you? Can you say tonight, in parting with the day that's slipping fast, that you helped a single brother of the many that you passed? Is a single heart rejoicing over what you did or said; Does the man whose hopes were fading, now with courage look ahead? Did you waste the day, or lose it? Was it well or sorely spent? Did you leave a trail of kindness, or a scar of discontent? As you close your eyes in slumber, do you think that God will say, "You have earned one more tomorrow by the work you did today?*

—John Hall

I rolled into 1998, trying to deal with my illnesses and to keep smiling to mask the pain and fear hidden within. My family begged me to leave Allen, but I truly loved him, even through the difficulty, although I spent more times angry at him than happy.

That fall, Allen and I took the boys hunting, and I noticed my pinky finger on my left hand kept going numb. I was so busy that I never dwelled on what the problem might be. I was currently enrolled in precalculus classes along with working twelve-hour shifts.

While I was driving to work one morning, I felt as if I was having a conversation with myself about being able to endure anything and not blaspheming the Lord like Job. I felt I also would be able to endure anything as long as my children were left alone. It was the first of many such conversations on those hour-long drives to and from work and a lesson that even if something were to happen to my children, I would come to know that God loved them and would care for them.

On the night before Veterans Day in November, I was getting ready for bed, and as I ran my finger across my chest to remove the bra strap, I felt a lump. Time seemed to go into slow motion as I traced the outline of the lump. It ran the width of two fingers from my nipple upward about the length of a finger, and I caught my breath. It had not been there that morning. I would have bet my life on it. I screamed for Allen and ran for the hall, where he met me, and as I grabbed hold of his hand, I told him to feel it and tell me what it was. I called in to work and went to my nurse practitioner the next day. The doctor scheduled me for a mammogram and ultrasound the following day. No one in my family had ever dealt with cancer, so I had no idea what I was facing. I drove myself over to the appointment in dread, knowing something was not right. My fears were confirmed when the technician called me back in for more ultrasound pictures. Then they put me in this room. Then a technician came in and explained the situation and recommended I go upstairs for a surgeon to immediately do a biopsy. The technician had to call my nurse practitioner to get the referral, but she had my husband sitting in her office needing more pain pills and complaining of possible kidney stones. I was informed that it was more important to come back and take him to the hospital for more tests, and so I headed home reluctantly. To this day, a part of me struggles with anger that if I would have had the biopsy done that day instead of a month later, I would not have had to endure as much as I did. I was then scheduled for a needle biopsy by the local ob-gyn, and when I went for my appointment, the doctor informed me that he was not capable of performing a needle biopsy. So I went in for a needle biopsy of the breast and left his office with a pap smear.

Next, I was scheduled with the local surgeon that covered two cities an hour's drive from each other, and when I went to my appointment, I was informed he would be late. I sat in the waiting room for two hours, waiting on him, and by the time he got there, everyone had left except a lady from administration. He came into the exam room, and after he heard why I was there, he took out a paper towel and started making notes and then asked if he could examine me. He did not speak English very well, and I had a hard time understanding what he was saying. Upon examination, he decided that the lump was scar tissue from a car accident I had had a year before and the seatbelt had bruised me. He explained that it did not feel like cancer and would just like to watch it for a bit. He went on to say he was in the process of moving from one city to the other and would have me make an appointment when the move was complete in a few weeks. I was living in a blur, trying to work, focusing on my college precalculus class, dealing with Allen's addiction, being a mom, and now trying not to fear what I was facing. I was not at peace with waiting and watching, and so I pursued the biopsy by calling and making an appointment for surgery. By the time I got it scheduled, we were already a month out from the date I had discovered the lump.

The nurse had a hard time hitting the vein in my hand for the IV and had me soaked in blood by the time I had enough and insisted she use the vein in the crook of my right arm. The anesthesiologist gave her an odd look when he entered. I was standing in a blood-soaked gown while she was changing the sheets, and then I had to change my gown. He went on to explain the surgeon was running late, and as soon as he got word the doctor was heading in our direction, he would start my medications. The surgeon was two hours late again, and after the surgery, he apologized for taking so much tissue out; however, he had been concerned by what he had seen during the procedure. The doctor said it looked like chicken fat with sand, and it was very deep. I was sent home and told the results would take about a week to get back.

That week was probably the longest of my life. I had scheduled time off from work before all of this to get ready for Christmas. Now I was trying to keep everything as normal as possible around the house and not let fear take over. I went back to work at the end of that week and started calling the doctor's office on Monday but could not get any answers. It took all day, and I finally was scheduled in the afternoon the next day to see the doctor and get the results. I left work thinking how two words could change my life forever: "It's cancer." That was not what I wanted to hear, but in my heart, I knew with dread that was what it was. I took the kids with me while Allen ran to drop John off at practice and hurry to meet us. I was sitting on the exam table when the doctor entered and immediately told me it was cancer after I had just told him I was waiting until my husband got there. I held up my hand for him to stop talking and asked again for him to wait until my husband had arrived.

Words cannot start to explain the emotions that sweep over a person who hears those words. I told him I wanted it out. I told him to take the breast or whatever it took, just get it out of me. The surgeon wished to schedule me for the next day, but I said I had my final test for precalculus class then. I needed to feel in control of a life that was quickly spiraling away. So we scheduled the procedure for the day after the final, and I went home to absorb it all. I had to call work and family and start making preparations. The doctor said he would consult with an oncologist and meet with me before the surgery to go over the details of the mastectomy. I was running through a fog when I went over the next day to take the final exam, and about halfway through, I paused to ask myself what I was doing and then just wrote down answers and left. I had a good enough grade without the final to pass the class and ended with a C-.

When I got home, my mom was there, hugged me tight, and said that out of her four daughters, I was the only one who could do this. She explained how the others would deny the disease until it killed them, try alternative stuff, or just take their lives before it got too bad, but she said that I would do what it took to fight to the end—the warrior in me refusing to give up. The next day, the plan was that I would take Daisy to school and stay for the art class I volunteered for, and after school, the neighbor would watch the three older kids until Allen got home. I should have known things never go according to plans. Broc woke up vomiting in the middle of the night and could not go to school; Daisy started crying as soon as I tried to leave her at school, and so we trusted my mom with Broc and Daisy while Allen, Cody, and I headed to meet the doctor. When we got to the doctor's office, he informed us he had discussed the situation with an oncologist and was going to just do a lumpectomy instead of mastectomy, and because he was a specialist, I trusted his advice without question.

I was still in a fog from anesthesia and hardly remembered the doctor coming in, but I asked him if I still had a nipple, not realizing how scared I had been of losing my breast until that moment. He said he was able to save it, although he took so much tissue that it did not look well. He also removed lymph nodes from under my arm to be tested to see if the cancer had already spread. I had a very restless night and was so afraid I would rip out stitches that I lay my left arm over my stomach and did not move it even to get dressed or comb my hair. I was released the next day.

I was scheduled to see the doctor on Monday to get the bandages off. When I got into the office, the nurse took my blood pressure on the left arm, the one from which the doctor had removed the lymph nodes, and it felt like my arm was going to explode. The pain was so intense. I learned later that a nurse is not supposed to take blood pressure on that arm and that this nurse should have known better. When the doctor arrived, I lay down on the exam table, and as he went to lift my arm above my head, my leg came up. I had not moved my arm all weekend, and it had frozen up, so he asked why I had not been using it and went on to scold me. He told me I should be walking the wall with my arm but never explained what that meant. I was still trying to absorb everything that was going on. I was sent home with the promise that the staff would contact me as soon as the results came in for the lymph nodes.

After we played phone tag for what seemed like eternity, I finally got the results. Out of the twenty nodes the surgeon had removed, I had one with cancer, so I would have to undergo chemotherapy along with radiation. From my understanding, chemotherapy treats the whole body, whereas radiation treats a specific area. The complete diagnosis of the breast was this: multifocal areas of infiltrating ductal carcinoma, grade three; extensive ductal carcinoma in situ, high-grade; focal lymphovascular invasion, meaning the tumor had spread outside the milk ducts and was in the blood vessels. That was the way I understood it, and I also understood that it was a fast-growing cancer in stage three out of four. Also the lymph nodes dissection was this: carcinoma metastatic to one of twenty lymph nodes.

The nurse told me she would schedule me to visit with an oncologist as soon as he had an opening in February. I decided to make my own calls, and so my nurse practitioner told me who to call. I scheduled my own appointments with the radiation doctor and oncologist right after the holidays and as close to the beginning of the year as possible. Two days before Christmas, I was at work, and my breast felt engorged. It was swollen. I was in pain, and it was very warm to the touch, so I kept trying to get an appointment with the surgeon to see what was wrong. They told me he was in surgery all day in another city. Then he would be coming to our town afterward and scheduled me at 3:30 p.m.

Right before I left work, my boss said he would be in town on Christmas Eve with Santa, visiting some kids, and he asked if it was okay to drop by and see my kids. He said Santa would bring them a candy cane but wanted to know their names, ages, and some of their likes so that he would be convincing that he knew them. I wrote it all down as I headed out the door. I got home, and the staff told me the doctor was running late and that they would call me when he was headed over. In the meantime, my breast felt like it was on fire. At 9:00 p.m., I got a call from the ER that told me he was headed over, and so I went to meet him. When he came into the room, he apologized for being so late. He said that he was so exhausted after his surgery he had gone home and taken a nap before he came in. He then informed me that I needed to be patient with him since he was almost moved to town. He then thanked me for letting him be my surgeon since it had been thirty years since he had dealt with breast cancer. I was horrified at this revelation. I discovered that doctors didn't tell you things like this because the only way they could get experience was to do the procedures. I learned to start asking lots of questions about their experience after this. After he examined me, he said the blood would be absorbed back into my system and I just needed to be patient. I could use ice packs and take ibuprofen for the pain until it got better.

I left there totally frustrated and called my nurse practitioner the next morning, which was Christmas Eve, and told her what was going on. She called back shortly with the name of a surgeon in Boise and said he was gathering all my files and looking them over and wanted to meet with me that day. There was a major snowstorm, but I headed off to see the new surgeon. By the time I got there, he was all by himself. Sitting on his couch were two gifts, one for his wife and one for his baby's first Christmas, and yet he had waited. He examined me and told me how to walk the wall to loosen my arm up from the frozen position it was still in and threatened physical therapy if I did not accomplish it. He drew pictures and explained everything in detail so that I understood what I was dealing with. After he looked at the mammogram and ultrasound, he said he would have removed the breast completely and recommended we still do the procedures. He said that I had been without any kind of treatment far too long for my aggressively growing cancer, so he told me to get chemotherapy as soon as possible. Then he would schedule the mastectomy three months in. Thankfully, I had taken it upon myself to schedule with the radiologist shortly after the New Year.

When I got home, it was well into Christmas Eve. I received a call from my boss telling me he was in town with Santa and wanted to stop by. I could not hold back the tears when he pulled into my driveway. He and Santa got out of their car and literally had to drag Santa's bag up the sidewalk and into the house. My kids' faces all pressed against the living room window as they stared in amazement. John was twelve, and Broc was ten. Daisy was seven, and Cody was only two years old. Then my boss went back to his car and brought in a couple of frozen turkeys my co-workers had donated. We spent the next hour with Santa handing out wrapped toys with the kids' names on each one, and then my boss took pictures of us as a family. I was thinking the same thing that he was, namely that this was probably my last Christmas with my kids. It turned out he had taken donations from all our co-workers, and then his wife had gotten a discount from a local toy store and selected each gift personally for my kids and wrapped them. I was so amazed by the love from my co-workers that the true meaning of Christmas had never hit home so hard.

Breast Cancer

Breast cancer is cancer that forms in the cells of the breasts. There are numerous types of breast cancer, but cancer that begins in the milk ducts (ductal carcinoma) is the most common type.

After skin cancer, breast cancer is the most common cancer diagnosed in women in the United States. Breast cancer can occur in both men and women, but it's far more common in women.

Public support for breast cancer awareness and research funding has helped improve the diagnosis and treatment of breast cancer. Breast cancer survival rates have increased and the number of deaths has been declining, thanks to a number of factors, such as earlier detection, new treatments, and a better understanding of the disease.

It's not clear what causes breast cancer. Doctors know that breast cancer occurs when some breast cells begin growing abnormally. These cells divide more rapidly than healthy cells do. The accumulating cells form a tumor that may spread (metastasize) through your breast to your lymph nodes or to other parts of your body.

Breast cancer most often begins with cells in the milk-producing ducts. Doctors call this type of breast cancer "invasive ductal carcinoma." Breast cancer may also begin in the milk glands known as lobules (invasive lobular carcinoma) within the breast.

Staging Breast Cancer

Once your doctor has diagnosed your breast cancer, he or she works to establish the extent (stage) of your cancer. Your cancer's stage helps determine your prognosis and the best treatment options. Complete information about your cancer's stage may not be available until after you undergo breast cancer surgery.

Breast cancer stages range from zero to four, with zero indicating cancer that is very small and noninvasive. Stage-four breast cancer, also called metastatic breast cancer, indicates cancer that has spread to other areas of the body.

Your doctor determines your breast cancer treatment options based on your type of breast cancer, its stage, whether the cancer cells are sensitive to hormones, your overall health, and your own preferences. Most women undergo surgery for breast cancer and also receive additional treatment, such as chemotherapy, hormone therapy, or radiation.

There are many options for breast cancer treatment, and you may feel overwhelmed as you make complex decisions about your treatment. Consider seeking a second opinion from a breast specialist in a breast center or clinic. Talk to other women who have faced the same decision.

Breast Cancer Surgery

Operations used to treat breast cancer include the following:

- **Removing the breast cancer (lumpectomy).** During the lumpectomy, which may be referred to as breast-sparing surgery or wide local excision, the surgeon removes the tumor and a small margin of surrounding healthy tissue. Lumpectomy is typically reserved for smaller tumors that are easily separated from the surrounding tissue.

- **Removing the entire breast (mastectomy).** Mastectomy is surgery to remove all of your breast tissue. Mastectomy can be simple, meaning the surgeon removes all of the breast tissue—the lobules, ducts, fatty tissue, and some skin, including the nipple and areola. Or mastectomy can be radical, meaning the underlying muscle of the chest wall is removed along with breast tissue and surrounding lymph nodes in the armpit. Radical mastectomies are less commonly done today. Some women may be able to undergo a skin-sparing mastectomy, which leaves the skin overlying the breast intact and may help with reconstruction options.

- **Removing one lymph node (sentinel node biopsy).** Breast cancer that spreads to the lymph nodes may spread to other areas of the body. Your surgeon determines which lymph node near your breast tumor receives the lymph drainage from your cancer. This lymph node is removed using a procedure called "sentinel node biopsy" and tested for breast cancer cells. If no cancer is found, the chance of finding cancer in any of the remaining lymph nodes is small, and no other nodes need to be removed.

- **Removing several lymph nodes (axillary lymph node dissection).** If cancer is found in the sentinel node, your surgeon may remove additional lymph nodes in your armpit. However, there is good evidence that removal of additional affected lymph nodes does not improve survival in cases of early breast cancer following a lumpectomy, chemotherapy, and whole-breast irradiation for tumors less than two inches (five centimeters) in size and in cases where the cancer has spread to just a few lymph nodes in the armpit. In such cases, chemotherapy and radiation treatment after the lumpectomy have proved to be equally effective. This avoids the serious side effects, including chronic swelling of the arm (lymphedema), that often occur after lymph node removal. However, axillary lymph node dissection may still be performed if the sentinel lymph node contains cancer following a mastectomy in the case of larger breast tumors or when a lymph node is large enough to be felt on physical exam. It may also be performed in situations when a woman elects to receive partial breast irradiation.

Radiation Therapy

Radiation therapy uses high-powered beams of energy, such as X-rays, to kill cancer cells. Radiation therapy is typically done using a large machine that aims the energy beams at your body (external beam radiation). But radiation can also be done by placing radioactive material inside your body (brachytherapy).

External beam radiation is commonly used after a lumpectomy for early-stage breast cancer. Doctors may also recommend radiation therapy after mastectomy for larger breast cancers. When external beam radiation is used after a woman has tested negative on a sentinel node biopsy, there is evidence that the chance of cancer occurring in other lymph nodes is significantly reduced.

Side effects of radiation therapy include fatigue and a sunburnlike rash where the radiation is aimed. Breast tissue may also appear swollen or more firm. Rarely, more serious problems may occur, including arm swelling (lymphedema), broken ribs, and damage to the lungs or nerves.

Chemotherapy

Chemotherapy uses drugs to destroy cancer cells. If your cancer has a high chance of returning or spreading to another part of your body, your doctor may recommend chemotherapy to decrease the chance that the cancer will recur. This is known as adjuvant systemic chemotherapy.

Chemotherapy is sometimes given before surgery in women with larger breast tumors. Doctors call this "neoadjuvant chemotherapy." The goal is to shrink a tumor to a size that makes it easier to remove with surgery. This may also increase the chance of finding a cure. Research is ongoing into neoadjuvant chemotherapy to determine who may benefit from this treatment.

Chemotherapy is also used in women whose cancer has already spread to other parts of the body. Chemotherapy may be recommended to try to control the cancer and decrease any symptoms the cancer is causing.

Chemotherapy side effects depend on the drugs you receive. Common side effects include hair loss, nausea, vomiting, fatigue, and a small increased risk of developing infection.

Hormone Therapy

Hormone therapy—perhaps more properly termed hormone-blocking therapy—is often used to treat breast cancers that are sensitive to hormones. Doctors sometimes refer to these cancers as estrogen-receptor positive (ER positive) and progesterone-receptor positive (PR positive) cancers.

Hormone therapy can be used after surgery or other treatments to decrease the chance of your cancer returning. If the cancer has already spread, hormone therapy may shrink and control it.

Treatments that can be used in hormone therapy include the following:

- **Medications that block hormones from attaching to cancer cells.** Tamoxifen is the most commonly used selective estrogen-receptor modulator (SERM). SERMs act by blocking estrogen from attaching to the estrogen receptor on the cancer cells, slowing the growth of tumors and killing tumor cells. Tamoxifen can be used in both pre—and postmenopausal women. Possible side effects include fatigue, hot flashes, night sweats, and vaginal dryness. More significant risks include cataracts, blood clots, stroke, and uterine cancer.

- **Medications that stop the body from making estrogen after menopause.** One group of drugs called aromatase inhibitors blocks the action of an enzyme that converts androgens in the body into estrogen. These drugs are effective only in postmenopausal women. Aromatase inhibitors include anastrozole (Arimidex), letrozole (Femara) and exemestane (Aromasin). Side effects of aromatase inhibitors include joint and muscle pain as well as an increased risk of bone thinning (osteoporosis). Another drug called fulvestrant (Faslodex) directly blocks estrogen, which keeps tumors from getting the estrogen they need to survive. Fulvestrant is generally used in postmenopausal women for whom other hormone-blocking therapy is not effective or who can't take tamoxifen. Side effects that may occur include fatigue, nausea, and hot flashes. Fulvestrant is given by injection once a month.

- **Surgery or medications to stop hormone production in the ovaries.** In premenopausal women, surgery to remove the ovaries or medications to stop the ovaries from making estrogen can be an effective hormonal treatment. This type of surgery is known as prophylactic oophorectomy and may be called surgical menopause.

Targeted Drugs

Targeted drug treatments attack specific abnormalities within cancer cells. Targeted drugs approved to treat breast cancer include the following:

- **Trastuzumab (Herceptin).** Some breast cancers make excessive amounts of a protein called human growth factor receptor 2 (HER2). Trastuzumab targets this protein, which helps breast cancer cells grow and survive. If your breast cancer cells make too much HER2, trastuzumab may help block that protein and cause the cancer cells to die. Side effects may include heart damage, headaches, and skin rashes.

- **Lapatinib (Tykerb).** Lapatinib targets the HER2 protein and is approved for use in advanced metastatic breast cancer. Lapatinib is reserved for women who have already tried trastuzumab and whose cancer has progressed. Potential side effects include nausea, vomiting, diarrhea, fatigue, mouth sores, skin rashes, and painful hands and feet.

- **Bevacizumab (Avastin).** Bevacizumab is a drug designed to stop the signals cancer cells use to attract new blood vessels. Without new blood vessels to bring oxygen and nutrients to the tumor, the cancer cells die. Possible side effects include fatigue, high blood pressure, mouth sores, headaches, slow wound healing, blood clots, heart damage, kidney damage, high blood pressure, and congestive heart failure. Research suggests that although this medication may help slow the growth of breast cancer, it doesn't appear to increase survival times. For this reason, bevacizumab isn't approved by the Food and Drug Administration to treat breast cancer. But doctors may prescribe it for what's known as off-label use. Use of bevacizumab in breast cancer is controversial. Side effects of targeted drugs depend on the drug you receive. Targeted drugs can be very expensive and aren't always covered by health insurance.

Clinical Trials

Clinical trials are used to test new and promising agents in the treatment of cancer. Clinical trials represent the cutting edge of cancer treatment, but by definition, they're unproven treatments that may or may not be superior to currently available therapies. Talk with your doctor about clinical trials to see if one is right for you.

Examples of treatments being studied in breast cancer clinical trials include the following:

- **New combinations of existing drugs.** Researchers are studying new ways of combining existing chemotherapy, hormone therapy, and targeted-therapy drugs. Testing new combinations may help determine if certain breast cancers are more susceptible to specific combinations.

- **Bone-building drugs to prevent breast cancer recurrence.** Previous research found that adding a bone-building drug to hormone therapy treatment after surgery for premenopausal women reduced the risk of breast cancer recurrence. The drug used in the study, zoledronic acid (Reclast and Zometa), is a type of drug called a bisphosphonate, which is used to treat bone loss (osteoporosis) and other bone diseases. The group of women who received zoledronic acid experienced fewer cancer recurrences than the group that didn't receive the drug during the study, which lasted four years. But newer studies haven't shown that zoledronic acid lessens the risk of recurrence for breast cancer.

- **Using higher doses of radiation over a shorter period of time on a smaller portion of the breast.** Researchers are studying partial breast irradiation in women who've undergone lumpectomy. Partial breast irradiation involves higher doses of radiation aimed at only a portion of the breast rather than the entire breast. Radiation used in partial breast irradiation can come from a machine outside your body, or it can come from tubes or catheters placed within the breast tissue.

A breast cancer diagnosis can be overwhelming. And just when you're trying to cope with the shock and the fears about your future, you're asked to make important decisions about your treatment.

Every woman finds her own way of coping with a breast cancer diagnosis.

CHAPTER 8

SAVING GRACE

Even though I was once a blasphemer and a persecutor and a violent man, I was shown mercy because I acted in ignorance and unbelief. The grace of our Lord was poured out on me abundantly, along with the faith and love that are in Christ Jesus. Here is a trustworthy saying that deserves full acceptance: Christ Jesus came into the world to save sinners—of whom I am the worst. But for that very reason I was shown mercy so that in me, the worst of sinners, *Christ Jesus might display His unlimited patience as an example for those who would believe on Him and receive eternal life.*

—1 Timothy 1:13-17 NIV

My year started out in a whirlwind meeting with the radiologist, who then set me up with an oncologist and immediately laid out my treatment plan. My doctor also referred me to a plastic surgeon for future work after I took chemo for three months and then underwent the mastectomy and finished up with three more months of chemo and six weeks of radiation. I had enough leave days saved up to take off work on the weeks I would do chemo, which would occur every three weeks. I went to my appointment at the plastic surgeon the day before treatment started, and while I was in the waiting room, a couple of ladies started talking to me. When they discovered I was to have my first chemo the next day, one of them said her friend, Brenda, was a masseuse and would love to stop by and massage my feet to help with nerves.

I had to be at the hospital early for surgery to have a port placed in my chest, and then I would go over to MSTI for the first treatment. The port was placed above my breast on the right side to make it easier to receive IV fluids. For the first chemo treatment, Brenda showed up and massaged my hands and feet. I had my treatment administered through the port. The nurses gave me Adriamycin. One of the side effects of this drug would affect me years later because it was weakening of the heart muscle. The risk of damage to the heart increases with the total amount of the drug administered. The paper listing all of the side effects that I signed also noted a periodic evaluation of heart function would be necessary in order to monitor this progression.

When I got home, I was feeling great and believed I was going to just blow through this so easily. My neighbor came over to check on me and told me to be ready, and sure enough, about five hours from leaving the hospital, I started heaving. Daisy had gone to her friend's house for the night, but the boys, all three, lay out on the living room floor and watched television as I lay on the couch. None of the antinausea medications worked, and it got so I would heave into a trash can. Then Allen would help me back up on the couch and clean the trash can. I ended up in the bathroom, hanging over the toilet and sleeping on the floor. At no time in my life, even through molestation, had I ever felt so powerless and weak. After two days of vomiting, I felt like I was floating or in a bubble. It's hard to describe. I finally got my appetite back and would eat everything I could find.

Allen was working for a lady named Maria and had explained everything to her and that he would have to work around my treatments. One night shortly after my first chemo when I was starting to feel better, I went to bed crying to the Lord, begging for His help because I had no idea how I was going to work to support the family, fight cancer, and raise kids. I was really concerned how I was going to feed them and deal with Allen's drug addiction, but worst of all, I didn't even know if I was going to live through it. The next morning,

Maria called and said she woke up crying with the family on her heart, and she said that she was supposed to feed us while I went through the treatments. Maria's church brought us meals every single night for three months. Most of the time, it was home-cooked food, and they brought me flowers, cards, hats and other personal items. The love of that church changed my life.

My parents and siblings made excuses that Allen wouldn't let them talk to me on the phone, but they made no effort to come by. And here were complete strangers serving the Lord by taking care of my family. I had been told that two weeks to the day of my first chemo, I would lose all my hair, so the day before, I went to a wig shop and tried on different ones. I could not decide on one, and I was delaying the inevitable. The next morning, two weeks to the day, while I was in the shower, I felt clumps of hair just fall out. There was no pain. It would just tumble to the ground. The kids thought it was cool and could not help but tug out hair in fascination. I couldn't cook because hair was getting into everything, so I decided Allen needed to shave my head. He cut what was left as short as possible and then shaved the rest. I laughed with them so the kids would not get scared, and then I went to take a bath and just bawled. That Sunday, I had to go to work. I still had not gotten a wig, so I wore a turban. I was so self-conscience but learned to look at myself in the mirror and see something I liked in my reflection before I headed out for work. Some days, I would have to place my nose against the mirror and tell myself I liked the sparkle in my eyes, but still, off to work I would go.

I had chemo every three weeks for three months, and each time, I fought the nausea with a different medicine until it came to me getting sick as soon as I would pull into the MSTI parking lot because of anxiety. The nurses had to inject a syringe full of Benadryl as they were accessing the port. It hit me so fast. As I watched the nurse squeezing the syringe, my eyes grew heavy, and I fell asleep. I would then take Ativan, an antianxiety medicine, for the next few days while I was at home and sleep most of the time.

At the end of the three months, my uterus started bleeding, and while I was seeing my surgeon to prepare for the mastectomy, I mentioned the bleeding. He had blood work done that showed I was extremely anemic and sent me directly over to my ob-gyn. He set me up for surgery after the weekend and told me not to move off the couch and keep my hips elevated. I was switching out blood-soaked pads every hour and feared I would need a blood transfusion before it was all over. I had an endometrial ablation and then had to have shots in my stomach every day for five days to get my white cell counts up for my immune system. One of the ladies from the church who brought over meals was a nurse, and so she gave me the needed shots as well as prayed with the family.

I wore a wig for the first three months but ran into trouble at work because I had to adjust it every time I came out of the acid hood, a place where we mixed and used chemicals under a ventilation system. When I was eating lunch in the cafeteria, it would start to slide, and I would have to run and fix it. I went in for the mastectomy on April 21 and then had to switch to a chemo that would not make me nauseous but would cause extreme bone pain. A week after the surgery and a day after the chemo, I attended the first Komen Race for the Cure held in Boise. My best friends from childhood had rallied a group from childhood that was there in support of me. They convinced me to lose the wig and wear the pink hat, so I turned it around backward and walked the race with all my friends and family. My eighty-year-old grandmother was to walk the one mile, but when we got to the turn point and I hugged her, she asked where I was going. When I told her I was walking the full five kilometers, she said that if I could do it so could she, and off we went. I was in tears when we crossed the finish line with my grandmother and mom on one side and daughter holding my hand on the other. The reality of what race I was truly running hit hard, and I hurt so badly from the chemo that later my legs would just tremble.

I had six weeks off work to heal and then started in with radiation along with the last of the chemo. I would work and then stop off for radiation and then drive on home every day and do chemo every three weeks on my day off. The radiation burned so badly I had third-degree burns and had to wear as baggy shirts as I could find. My boss decided to offer me a job that was five days a week with better hours to accommodate the radiation, and so I got a desk job in the engineering bull pen.

I learned to look at people's foreheads or chins so I didn't have to see what their eyes were saying, and then there were just the plain old obnoxious ones who said hurtful things without even thinking. One time, I was hurting something awful and had to grip the rail as I walked down the stairs. A couple of construction workers were standing at the bottom and staring. After I passed them, I heard one comment that he bet I could beat the other one up. Another time, I spent the day working with Allen. I had on a baggy shirt because I had only one breast, so it had become my new clothing option, and consequently, I had to run to the store. I got out of the vehicle, and as I was walking toward the store, two elderly ladies got out and stared at me. I could hear them discussing whether I was a male or female. My very being just wanted to flee, crawl back into my car, and go home and hide, but that is not how I handle things. So I sucked it up and went in the store, and just as I was about to go to the checkout, I noticed a man staring. I had enough by then, and I was going to give him a piece of my mind; however, just as I approached him, his wife stepped out from behind a shelf with really short hair. They both smiled, and he said not to worry, that it grows back.

I finished all the treatments by the end of June, and on my birthday in September, I took off the hat. On the first day back to work, I went without my head covered. As I stepped out of the lab, a group of guys came around the corner, and one of them smarted off that I had cut the hell out of my hair. I said no, that it was just starting to grow back. His buddies were trying to get him to shut up, but he kept on harassing as they followed me down the hall. The next day, he stopped off to apologize, and I told him he had no right to talk to anyone like that regardless of what they were going through. I continued lifting weights to keep my arm from freezing up and to feel better all the way around.

I then went to the church that had fed my family for three months to thank the congregation, and when I entered and met the pastor, I felt more at home than I had ever felt in my entire life. I had taken Cody with me, and we spent the service in the cry room; however, the pastor announced at the end of the service that I was there to thank the families that had served us. I started attending but some of the things the pastor talked about didn't make sense, so I would go home and call my grandma, and we would discuss the Bible. The New Life Christian Church in Emmett, Idaho, became my family, and I grew a hunger for the Word. For the first time ever, I started understanding the Bible. During the month of December, the pastor was reading the story of the birth of Christ. Broc and Daisy were sitting next to me with their Bibles opened, scanning the pages. Broc got all excited and informed me the story of Jesus' birth was in the Bible. I teared up when I realized how much I had failed my children. We have always celebrated Christmas, and I have nativity scenes all over the house, so I assumed my children understood the Bible story. I am so thankful it is never too late with the Lord, and my children were also saved. My walk with the Lord was just beginning, and the emotional wounds were to start healing. I had never understood that Jesus loved me and that all my sins were covered and that I didn't have to do things to earn His love. It would be a long walk with lots of setbacks, but I would learn the true meaning of God's saving grace and the fact that He never gives up on anyone. I was in my early thirties and still had not heard my father say the words "I love you" to me, so this was new to me to understand the Lord as my Father would love me. One of my first prayers I even asked God was if it was okay for me to tell Him I loved Him.

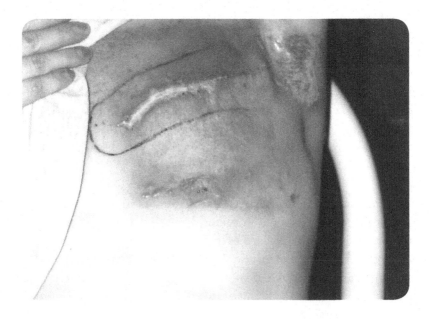

Endometrial Ablation

A procedure called endometrial ablation destroys the endometrium (the lining of your uterus) with the goal of reducing your menstrual flow. In some women, menstrual flow may stop completely. No incisions are needed for endometrial ablation. Your doctor inserts slender tools through your cervix (the passageway between your vagina and your uterus).

The tools vary, depending on the method used to destroy the endometrium. Some types of endometrial ablation use extreme cold, while other varieties depend on heated fluids, microwave energy, or high-energy radiofrequencies.

Some types of endometrial ablation can be done in your doctor's office, while others must be performed in an operating room. Factors like the size and condition of your uterus will help determine which endometrial ablation method is most appropriate.

Chapter 9

LEARNING THE CHRISTIAN WALK

There are more than a billion organisms in a teaspoon of soil. You'll change everything you encounter. The very ground is changed because you walked on it.

—Unknown

I continued to work, and during the spring of 2000, I scheduled to have the port and other breast removed and then start reconstruction. It was a three-hour surgery, and the surgeon removed the port. Then the plastic surgeon stepped in and started the reconstruction by just removing the nipple and cleaning out all the breast tissue from the right breast and then placing an expander under the muscle, leaving the skin hanging so the muscle would stretch to fit the skin. Then on the left side, the plastic surgeon brought the back muscle and skin around to replace the chest muscle that had been damaged by radiation and then placed an expander underneath. I was bandaged up and placed in a hospital room. I felt like a train had hit me. It took everything I had to even catch my breath.

I told the doctor not to give me a pain pill prescription because of Allen's addiction. Allen had to fold the mattress up. Then I would sit on the bed and lean against it, and he would lower it. To get up, I had to roll out onto my knees and then stand. I had three drainage tubes hanging out of my bandages.

I had been coaching Daisy's third—and fourth-grade girls' basketball team, and we were on the last week at this point. I told the girls on Tuesday's practice about the surgery, and Allen covered Thursday practice while I was in the hospital. I got up Saturday morning, and with Allen's help, I was able to shower and get to the basketball game, where I had to tell the girls not to hug me. One little girl brought in a picture she had colored and hidden in her shirt until she could give it to me. It was hard for these girls to not hug me when they got excited, and I had to run backward a few times to dodge them.

I had to have the pain prescription filled. One day after I woke up in excruciating pain, I needed to take one, but I noticed the bottle was half empty. I had only used a few, so I went out to the shop to ask Allen where the rest of my meds were and followed him to the house, where he pulled out a baggy with a bunch of pills. I took the baggy and the bottle and dumped it all down the toilet, deciding to breathe through the pain.

Once the bandages came off, I began stopping off by the doctor's office on my way home from work to get an injection of saline into the expanders until they slowly stretched the muscles out to form pockets as my right nipple area scarred over. I then had to have another surgery to have the expanders replaced by the implants. I had to retrain my muscles. You could poke my left chest, and I would feel it in my back. I couldn't open doors by pulling with my left arm and couldn't even complete one push up. I continued lifting weights, using the lat machine to dangle so my arm would extend and loosen the scar tissue. Up until then, I could hardly lift my left arm above my head, let alone extend it.

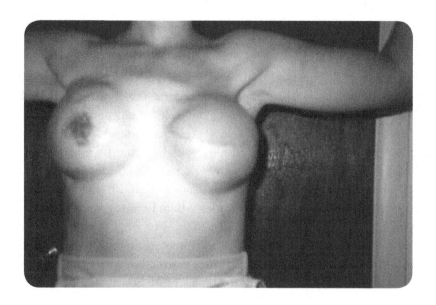

My sister, Faith, had a baby in July, and three months later, I flew to Missouri with my mom, Daisy, and Cody. My marriage was in so much trouble, but I didn't know how to fix it. A few days before I flew home, we were going to go shopping. I was just waiting for my paycheck to be deposited directly into the account. On payday, I called to verify it was there only to find it $500.00 short. I barely had enough money to get home, and when I went into work, I found an e-mail that a quick loan had taken me to court and got a judgment to garnish my wages in two segments. I was furious by the time I got home to confront Allen. He had hid all of this from me and was using my work and pay information for quick loans. I couldn't keep up with him anymore and told him to check into a rehab for help, or I was divorcing him.

One day at work, he called me in a desperation, his voice all shaky, and I told him I couldn't do it anymore and was not leaving work to save him and then hung up. Right before I got off work, I received a call from my childhood friend Angel at a rehab center. In desperation, Allen had called her, and she had gone and gotten him and driven him to a rehab, so I met them there. It was a Friday when he checked in, and I took the kids over to visit on the weekend. Then on Monday, he called and said they were releasing him. I was so in the dark about drugs that I did not understand the difference between detoxing and rehab, and he had only just detoxed.

I continued to go to church, and over time, God started changing me little by little. I was starting to understand that I am saved not by my actions but by the love of God, but still, I held onto the guilt of the affair. Then Allen insisted he was seeing a counselor to get better, and when he sat down at the table one night while I was going over bills and our lack of finances to cover them, he told me the counselor told him he needed the truth so that he could heal. I had doubts about him seeing a counselor but had no idea where he was going during that time frame and knew it was time for the lies to stop. If there was any chance of both of us healing, then all things needed to be laid out. So I admitted to that deceitful night, and we agreed to move on. The true healing was starting. There were to be no more lies.

Then I received a call at work from a gentleman wanting to come into the house and take pictures because my house was in foreclosure and up for sale in two weeks. I argued with him that he had the wrong number and went home to confront Allen. Turns out he had been taking back the checks I mailed for the house, knowing they would bounce because of my wage garnishment. He had also hidden the papers for the foreclosure and any correspondence from me. He borrowed the money from his dad to save our house just days before the foreclosure sale and pleaded with everyone that he had been rehabilitated and was no longer doing drugs.

Addiction to Prescription Pain Medications

No one decides to get addicted to prescription pain pills. Alienating family and friends, failing at work, and launching a small-time criminal career aren't what anyone plans on when they swallow their first Vicodin.

One in five Americans reports misusing a prescription drug at least once in his or her lifetime, but the overwhelming majority put the pills away with no lasting harm. So how does prescription painkiller abuse progress to full-blown opioid addiction?

For people with an inborn vulnerability to opioid addiction, taking pain pills can lead to an intoxicating rush that makes the brain want more. Repeating the high reinforces the cycle and sets the stage for drug addiction.

As an addiction-susceptible person uses opioids again and again, the reward system begins to wrongly learn these drugs are as essential to survival as food or water. Experts believe that the nerve cells of the brain actually undergo a change.

This explains the changes in behavior that go along with opioid addiction: neglecting responsibilities to family and friends, performing poorly at work, or losing interest in sex. Everyone's brain has a reward system, and millions of Americans use prescription pain pills—or even misuse them for a short time—without developing opioid addiction. What determines who becomes addicted and who doesn't?

Despite opioid drugs' reputation as "happy pills," not all people are wired to enjoy their effects. In many people, nausea and dizziness outweigh any euphoric rush from the drugs.

Even more people might experience pain pills like most people do alcohol. It's something pleasurable in moderation, but they have no urge to overdo it.

Studies show that about 5 to 10 percent of the population has brains that are already primed for addiction. Soon, they seek further chances to use the drug and increase the dose.

Still, certain factors are known to increase the risk for opioid addiction. Altogether, our genes account for 50 percent of the susceptibility to addiction. Studies of identical twins, who share the same genes, prove the link. If one identical twin develops a drug addiction, there's about a 50 percent chance the other twin will too.

That leaves half of the risk in the "environmental" category. This includes everything from your social group, your economic status, your family environment, and probably most importantly, stressful events during childhood.

Childhood trauma, such as physical or sexual abuse, losing a parent at a young age, or witnessing violent acts, create changes in the brain that last into adulthood. For reasons that aren't clear, these people are more prone to prescription drug abuse.

The most obvious environmental factor, though, is simply being around opioid drugs. For example, two teenagers might both be predisposed to opioid addiction. If one goes to a high school where prescription drug abuse is considered "cool," he might be more likely to use and become addicted. If the other teen is never exposed to opioid drugs, he may be more likely to stay clean.

Adults who have already abused other substances like alcohol or cocaine are more likely to fall victim to opioid addiction as well. Smokers and young people are at a higher risk. People with coexisting mental health conditions like depression, anxiety, and bipolar disorder are more likely to abuse drugs in general. The likelihood of serious opioid addiction also goes up depending on how long someone abuses the drug. Those who abuse prescription drugs for weeks have a better chance of overcoming drug addiction than people who abuse them continuously for years.

Whether or not someone is susceptible to opioid addiction depends on genes and early experiences. Studies have shown that when opiates are taken exactly as directed, they are safe, can manage pain effectively, and rarely cause addiction. When a person begins to experience signs of prescription pain medication abuse, he or she can avoid drug addiction—defined as the compulsive and uncontrolled use of drugs despite adverse consequences—by stopping use completely. But once true opioid addiction takes hold, the condition can be as firmly rooted as other chronic diseases like diabetes or high blood pressure, experts believe.

Even after they break free from physical dependence through a detox program, most people with opioid addiction relapse. They may need long-term maintenance therapy with methadone or Suboxone (buprenorphine/naloxone)—weaker opioids that prevent craving and withdrawal—along with counseling to break the cycle of detox and relapse.

Because of the biological basis for opioid addiction, condemnation and criticism are counterproductive, experts say. Although people often act hurtfully in the grip of opioid addiction, support from family, friends, and doctors is essential to their recovery.

Reconstruction Breast Surgery

Breast reconstruction is a surgical procedure that restores shape to your breast after a mastectomy (surgery that removes your breast to treat or prevent breast cancer). Breast reconstruction with flap surgery is a type of breast reconstruction that involves taking a section of tissue from one area of your body and relocating it to your chest to create a new breast mound.

Breast reconstruction with flap surgery is a complex procedure performed by a plastic surgeon. Much of the breast reconstruction using your body's own tissue can be accomplished at the time of your mastectomy. However, you'll need a second operation to achieve a correctly positioned, natural-appearing breast or to perform nipple reconstruction.

Chances are your new breasts won't look exactly like your natural ones used to. However, the contour of your new breasts can usually be restored so that your silhouette will look similar to your silhouette before surgery.

Breast reconstruction with flap surgery—using your body's own tissue to reconstruct your breast (autologous tissue reconstruction)—is the most complex reconstructive option. Your surgeon transfers a section of skin, muscle, fat, and blood vessels from one part of your body to your chest to create a new breast mound. In some cases, the skin and tissue need to be augmented with a breast implant to achieve the desired breast size.

Surgical Methods

Autologous tissue breast reconstruction uses one of two surgical methods:

- **Pedicle flap surgery.** The surgeon cuts some of the blood vessels nourishing the tissue to be transferred but keeps other blood vessels intact. Tunneling the tissue beneath your skin to your chest area, the surgeon then creates the new breast mound or pocket for the implant.

- **Free flap surgery.** The surgeon disconnects the tissue completely from its blood supply and uses microsurgical techniques to reattach the tissue flap to new blood vessels near your chest. Because of the intricate nature of reattaching blood vessels, free flap surgery typically takes longer to complete than pedicle flap surgery does. The recovery period for this type of surgery is longer too.

Types of Flap Surgery

The tissue for reconstructing your breast may come from your abdomen, back, or less commonly, your buttocks. Your surgeon determines which method is best for you based on your body type and your medical and surgical history, but they include the following:

- **Abdomen (TRAM flap).** Your surgeon removes tissue, including muscle, from your abdomen in a procedure known as a transverse rectus abdominal muscle (TRAM) flap. The TRAM flap can be transferred as a free flap or a pedicle flap. A pedicle TRAM flap is the only procedure that uses your whole rectus muscle—one of the four major muscles in your abdomen. If your surgeon performs a free-TRAM flap, only a portion of your rectus abdominal muscle is taken. In some instances, that portion of muscle may be very small. This is known as a muscle-sparing free-TRAM procedure. Using less of your muscle for reconstruction may help you retain abdominal strength after surgery.

- **Abdomen (DIEP flap).** Another type of abdominal procedure is the deep inferior epigastric perforator (DIEP) flap. This newer procedure is almost the same as a muscle-sparing free-TRAM flap, but skin and fat are the only tissues removed. Minimal abdominal muscle tissue is taken to form the new breast mound. A DIEP flap uses a free-flap approach. An advantage to this type of breast reconstruction is that you'll retain more strength in your abdomen. If your surgeon can't perform a DIEP-flap procedure for anatomical reasons, he or she might opt for the muscle-sparing free-TRAM flap instead. A variation of the DIEP flap, the superficial inferior epigastric artery (SIEA) flap, uses the same abdominal tissue but relies on blood vessels that aren't located so deeply within the abdomen. This provides a less invasive option for free-flap surgery. However, not all women have adequate SIEA blood vessels to make them good candidates for this type of flap surgery.

- **Back (latissimus dorsi flap).** Another surgical technique takes tissue, including skin, fat, and muscle, from your upper back. This is called a latissimus dorsi flap. The tissue is tunneled under your skin to your chest. Because the amount of skin and other tissue is generally smaller than in a TRAM-flap surgery, this approach may be used for reconstructing small and medium-sized breasts or for creating a pocket for a breast implant. Although it's not very common, some women experience muscle weakness in the back, shoulder, or arm after this surgery.

- **Buttocks (gluteal flap).** A gluteal flap is a free-flap procedure that takes tissue, possibly including muscle, from your buttocks and transplants it to your chest area. A gluteal flap may be an option for women who prefer tissue reconstruction but who don't have enough extra tissue in their backs or abdomens for those to serve as the tissue donor sites. Because adequate blood supply is critical to the survival of transplanted tissue in flap surgery, your surgeon may prefer not to perform a pedicle flap procedure if you're a smoker or if you have diabetes, vascular disease, or a connective tissue disorder. Also, obesity may preclude you from having a pedicle TRAM flap.

In general, autologous breast reconstruction is more extensive than a mastectomy or implant reconstruction is. Flap procedures result in larger incisions that take longer to heal and may require a longer hospital stay.

Nipple Reconstruction

Breast reconstruction may also entail reconstruction of your nipple (if you choose), including tattooing to define the dark area of skin surrounding your nipple (areola).

CHAPTER 10

FINDING FORGIVENESS

The Lord is my shepherd, I shall not be in want, He makes me lie down in green pastures, he leads me beside quiet waters, he restores my soul. He guides me in paths of righteousness for his name's sake. Even though I walk through the valley of the shadow of death, I will fear no evil, for you are with me, your rod and your staff, they comfort me. You prepare a table before me in the presence of my enemies. You anoint my head with oil, my cup overflows. Surely goodness and love will follow me all the days of my life and I will dwell in the house of the Lord forever.

—Psalm 23

The New Year brought hope that life was going to turn around, so Allen and I were baptized at the church. Allen was bitten by the cat and ended up going to the ER for shots and medication. He denied that he was given pain pills, but old doubts kept reeling their ugly heads for me.

I started waking up to a tapping feeling, and when I would open my eyes, it appeared to be a little girl standing beside my bed; however, I didn't feel any fear. This went on every night for about three or four days, and then one night, I had a dream where I was holding the little girl's hand as this bright light approached. It was as if we were standing on railroad tracks and a train was bearing down on us. Only the light was brighter than anything I had ever seen, and I could not stare at it directly. All of a sudden, I was shoved by the light, and it left with the girl. After I was born again and then baptized, I believe God was showing me that my baby girl I had miscarried was now with Him in heaven so that I would forgive myself. He also showed me that He didn't take me because I was not finished with His plans for me. Also around this time frame, I was driving home from work and felt a conversation going with the Lord. These conversations were not really a verbal but a heart conversation, something I have a hard time describing. I told him I was healed, and then He showed me a small black spot on my heart and turned my head to the left. At that very instant I was driving past the turnoff that led to Uncle Alvah's house. Then He told me that I had to forgive Uncle Alvah before I could heal completely.

Things lined up with my grandmother getting ill and having to go live with Uncle Alvah and his wife. I needed to go see her, and when I entered Uncle Alvah's house and visited with my grandmother, the Lord revealed to me that he was no longer a beast/devil but a pitiful old man. I left there with some power over the fear and the knowledge that the remainder of my heart would heal in time. I realized that forgiving people takes the power they hold away and life can get better.

We coached Daisy's basketball team, and toward the end, I started having trouble standing back up after leaning over to pick up a ball. Then the kids got me a bicycle for Mother's Day, and Allen and I would go for rides; however, I soon discovered I had no strength to pedal uphill. Then there was a five-kilometer run that Daisy and I had decided to run, and she left me in the dust. Soon, I had a very elderly gentleman pass me and give me encouragement. I knew something was definitely wrong by this point. When I finally reached the finish line and Daisy was there all red-faced because she had run the whole 5K, we went into all the booths. I lay on the chiropractors table, and after a little work, he informed me that my hips were out of alignment and I needed to come to his office. I started going and having him work on my back and hips, but after a time, I would leave his office in tears. It hurt so badly. I told my oncologist, who ordered a bone scan that came back negative, and yet I continued to hurt. So I went and saw my radiation doctor, who ordered an MRI of the lower back. I received a call at work the next day that the MRI showed a compression fracture and cancer in the L3 region. She had scheduled me for a bone biopsy the next day. I was numb from the waist down, and as I lay on my stomach, I could feel the chipping of the bone. The biopsy came back positive. My breast cancer cells had metastasized to the bone, and so I went through six weeks of radiation on L3. There was no blistering this time, but just a dark square patch remained.

At the end of the radiation, I wanted to show Allen how I appreciated that he had chosen family over his drug addiction. So we went on a mini vacation with the kids. Before we left, Allen was having tooth pain, so he got up early to see the dentist in emergency. Then Cody was sick, and I was exhausted from the radiation. The trip wasn't as relaxing as we had hoped, and I kept questioning Allen if he was on something; however, he denied it. After I had lived with his addiction for five years, now I could pinpoint when he wasn't quite right but still believed him when he denied it. He would look me in the eye and say that as bad as the withdrawals were last winter, he would never go through that again. My suspicions were answered when I discovered he was going to the dentist to get pain meds and was actually digging at his teeth with a tooth pick to crack them. The dentist finally said he would not see Allen anymore, and then our nurse practitioner said the same thing. I discovered he had been bouncing around from doctor and dentist offices and getting twenty to thirty hydrocodone every three to four days. I woke up one night shortly after I had confessed the infidelity to him sitting on the edge of the bed, and he gave me the chills because he was contemplating taking my life. It was the one and only time I was truly fearful of him. I am sure I was feeling this because of the old scars and the guilt I had carried. We had hurt each other so immensely, and we didn't know how to fix it.

I went in for the nipple reconstruction and only had tattooing after this was complete. The procedure did not work as well as planned, and with the cancer back, I was advised that surgery would weaken my immune, so I quit with the reconstruction process and left my chest as it was, one small little nub on the left and nothing on the right for nipples. Toward the end of the year, I was hurting again and could hardly walk, so the doctors had another MRI done of the area I was complaining about. They discovered the cancer had spread above and below the previous spot, and so they started me on six weeks of radiation immediately and also six months of chemo again. This chemo would not make me sick but would cause excruciating pain, bone chills, and hair loss. The pain was so severe at times my legs would just quiver, and the cold go so deep all I could do was soak in hot bathwater or lay on heating pads.

I also discovered that Daisy was flunking fifth grade, and the administration planned on holding her back the following year. Broc was flunking eighth grade and hanging with a bad crowd known for experimenting with drugs. I pulled them both out of school to homeschool. It was getting harder and harder for me to come home from work, especially on days when I would walk in the door exhausted only to find Allen sitting on the couch and glaring at me and then start questioning which co-worker I took to the motel for lunch this time. Trust was no longer a part of our marriage. I did not care for sex any longer, but then he would get angry that I was not fulfilling my wifely duties. If I did not attend our weekly scheduled time, he would go in the boy's bedroom and harass them. I was learning to walk with God every day but hadn't quite learned the knack of giving Him all my problems. We stopped being a family, and everyone did what they could to survive. The boys hid out in their bedrooms. Daisy went to friends' houses. Allen slept on the couch all day, and when I wasn't working, I wished I was. If not for the love of my children, I would have walked out the door.

Metastatic Cancer—Stage IV

Bone metastasis occurs when cancer cells spread from their original site to a bone. Nearly all types of cancer can spread (metastasize) to the bones. But some types of cancer are particularly likely to spread to bone, including breast cancer and prostate cancer.

Bone metastasis can occur in any bone but more commonly occurs in the pelvis and spine. Bone metastasis may be the first sign that you have cancer, or bone metastasis may occur years after cancer treatment.

Bone metastasis can cause pain and broken bones. *With rare exceptions, cancer that has spread to the bones can't be cured. Treatments can help reduce pain and other symptoms of bone metastases.*

Medications

Medications used for people with bone metastasis include the following:

- **Bone-building medications.** Drugs commonly used to treat people with thinning bones (osteoporosis) may also help people with bone metastasis. These medications can strengthen bones and reduce the pain caused by bone metastasis, reducing the need for strong pain medications. Bone-building medications may also reduce your risk of developing new bone metastasis. These drugs can be administered every few weeks through a vein in your arm or through an injection. Bone-building medications can cause temporary bone pain and kidney problems. They increase your risk of a rare but serious deterioration of your jawbone (avascular osteonecrosis).

- **Chemotherapy.** If cancer has spread to multiple bones, your doctor may recommend chemotherapy. Chemotherapy travels throughout your body to fight cancer cells. Chemotherapy can be taken as a pill, administered through a vein, or given both ways. Side effects depend on the specific chemotherapy drugs you are given.

- **Hormone therapy.** For cancers that are sensitive to hormones in the body, treatment to suppress those hormones may be an option. Breast cancers and prostate cancers are often sensitive to hormone-blocking treatments. Hormone therapy can involve taking medications to lower natural hormone levels or medications that block the interaction between hormones and cancer cells. Another option is surgery to remove hormone-producing organs—the ovaries in women and the testes in men.

- **Pain medications.** Pain medications may control the pain caused by bone metastasis. Pain medications may include over-the-counter pain relievers, such as ibuprofen (Advil, Motrin, and others) or strong prescription pain relievers, such as morphine (Avinza, MS Contin, and others). It may take time to determine what combination of pain medications works best for you. If you're taking medications but still experiencing pain, tell your doctor.

External Radiation Therapy

Radiation therapy uses high-powered energy beams, such as X-rays, to kill cancer cells. Radiation therapy may be an option if your bone metastasis is causing pain that isn't controlled with pain medications. Depending on your situation, radiation to the bone can be administered in one large dose or several smaller doses over many days. Side effects of radiation depend on the site being treated. In general, radiation therapy causes skin redness and fatigue.

Coping with bone metastasis requires more than enduring bone pain. It also involves coming to terms with the news that your cancer has spread beyond its original site. Cancer that has metastasized can be very difficult to cure, though people can live several years with bone metastasis. Your doctor will work to minimize your pain and to maintain your function so that you can continue your daily activities.

Each person finds his or her own way to cope with a cancer diagnosis. Until you find what works best for you, consider trying to these mechanisms:

- **Find out enough about bone metastasis to make decisions about your care.** Ask your doctor about the details of your cancer and your treatment options. Ask about trusted sources of further information. If you do research on your own, good places to start include the National Cancer Institute and the American Cancer Society.

- **Find someone to talk with.** Although friends and family can be your best allies, they may have difficulty coping with the shock of your diagnosis. In these cases, talking with a counselor, medical social worker, or a pastoral or religious counselor can be helpful. Ask your doctor for a referral.

- **Connect with other cancer survivors.** You may find comfort in talking with other cancer survivors. Cancer survivors can provide unique insight into your situation. Contact your local chapter of the American Cancer Society to find cancer support groups in your area.

- **Come to terms with your illness.** Coming to terms with the fact that your cancer may no longer be curable can be difficult. For some people, having a strong faith or a sense of something greater than themselves makes this process easier. Others seek counseling from someone who understands life-threatening illnesses, such as a medical social worker, psychologist, or chaplain. Many people also take steps to ensure that their end-of-life wishes are known and respected by writing down their wishes and discussing them with their loved ones.

Chapter 11

Metastasized

Praise the Lord, O my soul, and forget not all his benefits who forgives all your sins and heals all your diseases, who redeems your life from the pit and crowns you with love and compassion, who satisfies your desires with good things so that your youth is renewed like the eagle's.

—Psalm 103:2-5

The year started out with me homeschooling the two kids and going to work and then having radiation on my way home. I had a CT scan in January to make sure the cancer hadn't spread to any of the organs.

I found out much later from the kids and my neighbor that Allen would pretend to leave for work before me and then come back as soon as I pulled out of the driveway. He would sleep all day and then go out before I got home and arrive after me, pretending as if he had worked all day. The kids were threatened with grounding if they told me, and so the distance in the relationship with my kids just kept growing.

I had to have surgery to get a port placed back into my chest and had to get chemo every three weeks. I lost my hair again, but this time, the style was a certain kind of hat, so I just got a bunch of different colors to match my outfits and wore them instead of even trying to find a wig. My eyebrows thinned but never fell out this time either. As a family, we taught Sunday school for two—and three-year-olds, and I was concerned that losing my hair would terrify the little ones. I tried to give my notice, but the church leaders insisted the children would be fine. I was so amazed at how wonderful they actually were. One little girl took my hat off and kissed my head, which brought tears to my eyes.

We also coached Cody's T-ball team, and I rediscovered how being around little ones definitely healed the heart. I talked to Broc and told him if he would change the group of friends he was hanging with and buckle down on school, I would help him pursue whatever dream he wanted, and he chose rodeo. So after I homeschooled him for the remainder of eighth grade, I got him signed up for high school rodeo club, and he started bull-riding along with bareback. Daisy was still struggling with math at the end of fifth grade, so I geared up to homeschool her whole sixth-grade school year.

At the end of my chemo, I was still hurting so badly that I could barely walk, and when I was getting up from my seat at work, it took me a while to straighten out. I would then have to hold the wall for stability. So doctors performed another MRI, this time not just around the painful areas but from neck down through the pelvis, and it showed a spot in my neck in the cervical area and massive amounts of lesions in the pelvic bone. They could radiate the neck but could not do anything for the pelvic area except start me on this experimental hormonal blocker infusion treatment, Herceptin, one-third dose every week and then also a bone treatment called Areidia every four weeks and an implant placed in the skin in my stomach, Zoladex, to shut down my ovaries every twelve weeks. The outlook looked pretty poor, and the doctor signed paperwork stating I was terminal. I was given less than a year to live.

Around this same time, I discovered Allen was hiding mail again, especially the bank statements, which meant he was seeing doctors and back on pain meds and using quick loans to cover the cost. I took a draw on my life insurance to get bills under control and take the family to Disneyland and try to live as stress-free as possible for my last year. My employer set me up to work from home by providing a computer. After I finished the six weeks of radiation on my neck, we headed to California. The kids thought they were just on vacation, but I knew this was it for the time with my family.

I met a lady at church and felt drawn to her. Joy called one evening after we had just met and said she had heard my story and wanted to help in some way. After some discussion, I discovered she could give massages, and I desperately needed them. We arranged to meet at her house once a week, and Daisy would babysit while she massaged and made me mobile again. Not only did a friendship blossom, but we forged a sisterhood in the Lord.

Broc was signed up for high school rodeo, which would also hold him accountable with his grades, and began to learn bull—and bareback-riding. Daisy was homeschooled and went with me to all my weekly treatments. We would crawl into the hospital bed together and watch cartoons or take a nap. Daisy was shown where the drinks and snacks were and became my little helper. It was not how I would have chosen to bond with my daughter, but it worked. John did his best to excel at school and sports and was also working and keeping busy so as not to face what was going on at home, and Cody was Allen's little buddy.

I used the life insurance draw to pay cash for Allen a slightly used truck and then a little more to pay for adding an office room onto our house and get the remodeling done I so desperately wanted. I put the money in the savings, and after a long discussion about responsibility and taking care of the family, I trusted Allen with it. I would not be around in a year, and he needed to step up for the family.

Before long, Allen started going to the ER on a regular basis again until I finally told him I would not go get him anymore and that he should not call me from the ER again. He had surgery for kidney stones and then called the doctor at his house because the pharmacy would not give him more pain meds and threatened the doctor. I could hear him calling into work that he had been up with me all night or had me at the ER and then go fall asleep on the couch. When I would ask why he was not at work, he would tell me there wasn't anything going on that day. He tore all the siding off our house and bought the new stuff, but it sat out in the yard for over a year before he would put it on. At Christmas, he was to take some money out of the savings account to get the boys' chaps paid for, and he kept postponing doing it. I kept questioning him about the money in savings, but he insisted it was all still there. He got the chaps home, so I let it slide. The Herceptin infusion I had to get weekly made me feel like I had the flu. I was extremely tired for a day or two afterward, but otherwise, I was coping well. I just didn't have the energy to deal with the financial aspects, and I was trying to trust Allen.

CHAPTER 12

ENOUGH ALREADY

He gives strength to the weary and increases the power of the weak. Even youths grow tired and weary, and young men stumble and fall.
—Isaiah 40:29-30

My primary sclerosing cholangitis and ulcerative colitis were doing well on the meds, and I continued to coast along on the current treatments. I was still having problems with residual chemo in my brain, and I would forget things. One day, I couldn't remember my password to get on my work computer, and I messed it up. I tried to reboot it and ended up having to take it to work for the technicians to put a work order on it, which took a week. The doctor decided it was time for me to go on disability. I was trying to sleep during the days, which was exhausting, and sitting for long periods made my back and hips ache.

I had to go on pain meds, and being home, I was able to monitor Allen's activities better. He was not going to work as often as he had led me to believe previously. He was finding reasons to still go to the ER. He even shot a nail through his hand and had to have surgery. Then my pain meds started disappearing, a few at first and then half a bottle. He denied it and accused my older boys. One time, he handed me the bottle, which was full of white powder, and told me he had accidentally knocked it off the desk and stepped on it. I was sure he had switched the pills out with something else and then stomped on the bottle. Another time I went to take a pill and noticed they looked different, and when I questioned him, he admitted he had switched them out with some other safe medication. However, he was able to convince me that one of my boys may have been the one stealing the pain meds. I had never met anyone who was so good at playing mind games, and I was losing the battle.

I felt like I was losing my mind, and when I would confront him, he would not only deny it but also throw my infidelity in my face, even though we had agreed to speak of it no more. I had to start placing my pain meds under lock and key, but it still bothered me that Allen blamed the boys. I wanted out of my marriage so desperately but was part of a church now and trusted God to show me the way, and right now, it was to stay in my marriage

I told Allen I wanted to get a camper trailer because with my back, I could not sleep on the ground any longer on our camping trips. He fought it when I told him I planned on using the truck I had bought him as collateral until I finally told him I was going to do it. I was not ready for what I discovered when I went in and filed for the loan. I discovered that six months prior during Christmas, he had title-loaned the truck because he had used up the thousands of dollars in savings and needed to pay for the chaps for the kids and was paying $400.00 a month on interest ever since. So my loan for the trailer ended up paying off the title loan and made the payments $300.00 a month for the truck and trailer, saving us a $100 a month and getting a camper trailer.

Scar tissue had built up so badly on my chest that my range of motion was limited, and so I started seeing a physical therapist for some work to loosen things up. Allen had been really verbally picking at me and the boys, and I discovered he had pawned ten guns in the past six months. He had been missing work and vomiting a lot and sleeping most of the day, and I could not get away from him, not even to go to the restroom. He would follow me.

We got to spend some fun family time camping, and on one trip, we decided to walk into Loon Lake to see the old airplane wreckage. It was supposed to be a three-mile walk each way, so I stressed to the kids to take hiking shoes. When we got to the trail head, we discovered the short route was closed due to fire, and so we decided to take the long route, which turned out to be seven miles each way. Partway into the hike, Daisy had blisters so badly from the new boots she decided to wear, and because we wore the same size, I switched with her for my tennis shoes. By the time we got to the lake, I had blisters so awful I couldn't walk with the boots on. I was exhausted from the hike, and I did not know how I was going to make it out of there. Allen took the kids on to see the wreckage, and I lay down for a nap alongside the lake. When the guys got back, we headed out. Only I chose to go barefoot because I could not get the boots back on. I hiked the whole seven miles out barefoot.

I then discovered the Toyota title was missing from our security box in our office, but Allen kept denying title-loaning it, so I started meeting with the pastor for counseling. He told me to quit trying to be Allen's angel and to fix things every time he messed up. The pastor told me to get out of the way so that God could deal with Allen. With me being home, Allen decided that he wanted to go back to school and signed up with a local tech school. He told me he was working and then going to his brother's to shower and change before he went to school, and then he was coming home late.

The cancer was in my pelvic area throughout the bone, but Allen insisted that I perform my wifely duties weekly. So on Mondays, I could not even get out of bed I hurt so badly. My kids gave me so much happiness and made life worth fighting for, and a year came and went from my last diagnosis. My weekly treatments became once every three weeks, and my four-week Areidia turned into Zometa every twelve weeks. I had to continue stretching out and trying to exercise to keep scar tissue from binding up, and Joy continued to give massages to keep me mobile. I would have been bedridden had it not been for Joy.

By fall, I was so obsessed with Allen taking my pain meds and not admitting it that I questioned the boys one last time and then confronted Allen in front of them. He punched a hole in the wall and showed me the first sign that his addiction was escalating and that he was getting ready to get physical, and still, God would not release me. Allen started snorting his Copenhagen and using nose sprays often, which was something new, and my family begged me to leave him; however, they had not been around during my chemotherapy to see how he had taken care of me. Yes, he took my pain meds, and yes, I worked to support us; however, he held me and cleaned up after my messy vomiting and did the best he could with the kids. My dad had seen me bald once in the beginning and never came back around until my hair had grown back, and he lived just a few miles away. My mom and sister tried to convince me Allen was poisoning me, which grew a seed of suspicion for me.

By September, I was having major headaches and couldn't help but fear the cancer had moved to my brain, and dealing with all the chaos in the house was taking its toll. Allen was to sell the Toyota for a down payment on a car for John, and he still insisted it was not title-loaned. Then he forced Broc to refinish the stock on a gun. Allen grounded him time and again until it was done. Once the gun was finished, it disappeared. I discovered later he had pawned it along with most of the remaining tools he had. Broc did not get to go hunting that year.

I was having severe bouts of pain, causing me to lose control and cry, and Allen started accusing me of lying; however, he wouldn't tell me about what and insisted I take a lie detector test. I hadn't lied to him except for the one-night affair, and we had agreed to put it behind us. Broc had worked all summer for Allen at $5.00 an hour, but when it came time to pay Broc for the fifty-five hours he had put in, Allen gave him $20.00 and patted him on the back, telling him how proud he was of him. I later discovered that Allen had billed his boss for all of Broc's hours and kept the money.

My birthday came and went without anyone in the house even wishing me a happy birthday; however, Joy made me a cake, and her two children sang to me. I started having nightmares and feeling attacked spiritually, but by praying immediately, I would find peace. And then Allen started trying to convince me I was addicted to my pain meds. I had to keep them locked up so he couldn't get into them, and he was trying to turn it around that I was the addict. This constant emotional battle was wearing me down, and by November, Allen was having problems with not going to work again, so he told me he had quit and had gotten another job lined up. Shortly after, I discovered John's muscle relaxers were missing along with the Ativan I had used for my chemo treatments. He was back to lying around the house all day and having mood swings, which meant the boys and I had to deal with verbal abuse.

He said he lost the key to the gun closet, so I could not even see what, if any guns we even had left, and now I realized how much my energy level was diminished. What used to take me an hour or so to accomplish now took all day. I knew things could not continue as they were, or I would not be around much longer. It was taking everything I had to get out of bed every morning.

That Christmas, the family was all supposed to go see Allen's mom because she was not faring well, but at the last minute, he backed out, saying he had to work, so I headed out with the three younger kids. We spent the night at my mom's and visited his mother the next day. She was not doing well at all, and it was the last time we would get to see her. When I got home, John said Allen was home by 10:00 a.m. before he had left for work.

Also around this time, the dryer was acting up, and Allen reached under it and pulled out a syringe full of some kind of brownish liquid and an uncovered needle. I figured it was drugs and didn't have the energy to deal with it, so I threw it in the garbage. He tried to convince me it was something my nephew or sister had hidden at our house while he or she had been visiting. I should have dumped it down the toilet, but I wasn't thinking clearly. I was so angry that something like that was in my house, where my children could have gotten ahold of it. Some days, I felt like I was drowning and couldn't come up for air.

CHAPTER 13

DIVORCE

But those who hope in the Lord will renew their strength. They will soar on wings like eagles; they will run and not grow weary, they will walk and not be faint.

—Isaiah 40:31

The New Year came in with Allen having to go to Palm Springs for work and me running the little kids' wrestling program, which usually had sixty or so kids from kindergarten to eighth grade, and Cody was one of them. John was a senior and getting his college stuff together. Broc was rodeoing, and Daisy was in the junior high dance program and back in school in the seventh grade. Allen drove the first trip and commuted with the other employees. While there, he called home and told me stories how undercover cops investigating his coworkers for drugs and how the others had gotten busted, and then he told a story about his roommate bringing a woman home and slept with her with him in the room. I believed otherwise because all of a sudden, my prayers were answered, and the phone started ringing.

Allen's old boss called wanting the title to the Toyota he had bought from my husband last fall, and Allen had told him it was in a safety deposit box. His brother called wanting the tools he had loaned Allen, but I knew he had pawned it all. The title loan place called and said they had been lenient on collecting the Toyota because Allen had told them I had been in the hospital, fighting for my life, and lastly, the school that he had supposedly been attending for the past year sent a letter requesting payment because he had quit going during the summer. His brother told me that Allen had never come to his house to shower for school and that he did not see his brother the past summer. I received all this information in a matter of hours. On top of it, I realized that I could crawl out of bed on Monday morning without hurting and that being a wife to Allen was killing me slowly and very painfully, both physically and emotionally.

I had a wrestling tournament with over 250 kids on the morning Allen returned from Palm Spring, and there was no joy at his return. We both even said that neither of us had missed the other while we had been apart, and we knew our marriage was in trouble. He was home for less than a week and had to go back to finish the job; however, this time, he was flying, and the night before he flew out, I made a special family dinner. Only he got up from the table and spent the evening vomiting in the bathroom.

After he flew out, I started watching TV with the kids, and we laughed like I hadn't heard in years. When I asked the boys why, they said that they weren't allowed in the living room to watch TV as part of the family. Stunned, I then realized how messed up my family had become. The older boys were never allowed to watch TV when Allen was there, and I had given up fighting with him and complied. Allen called, and when I said good-bye and hung up without saying I loved him, he immediately called back and demanded to know what was wrong. I said good-bye and hung up again, and he called back fifteen times before I unplugged the phone.

I filed for divorce the next day without telling anyone until I had met with the lawyer and started the proceedings. I then had to tell the kids. The older two seemed relieved, but the younger two had no idea why. Then Allen went crazy and called all my friends and told them the pain meds I was on had made me lose my mind, and so they were all calling to check up on me. I had my brother break into the gun closet only to discover every single one of the guns was gone, including all the ones that had been birthday and Christmas presents for the kids, including scopes. Cody had gotten a scope for his gun for Christmas just a few months prior, and it also was gone. I also discovered he had been taking money from both boys because they had jobs. I knew I had gone about the divorce very poorly, but I wanted that man out of my life and did not want to face him and his lies one more minute. I felt as if my life and sanity depended on it.

He flew back and stayed at a hotel in Boise, and then his father and brother got involved and drove the kids and truck to him. The kids stayed the weekend with him, and Daisy came home furious. Allen told her all about my infidelity and informed the kids I was not safe to be around because of my medications, but in order to stay alive, I had to take them. He knew my faith and honestly believed I would not divorce him. Allen had called the pastor and Brad, one of the seniors of our church who then got involved.

I used the tax return to pay off the Toyota title loan and called Allen's old boss to meet me there to get the title. A divorce proceeding that should have been over in a few months dragged on with us being ordered into mediation. I told the church that if Allen would check himself into a rehab for more than a month, I would hold off on the divorce, but he refused and tried to convince me he attended an AA meeting and that he had no drug problem. To stall the mediation, he would call and cancel and dragged things out, and in the meantime, he paid nothing, not even the insurance on his own truck he was driving.

I ended up in the hospital ER with what the doctor guessed to be pancreatitis, and then at treatment, my blood test wouldn't clot, so the nurse had to dilute my meds and take much longer to administer them. The stress was taking its toll on my health or what health I had left. Allen was telling the kids that even my closest friends were angry at me for doing this, and I started to feel isolated and alone. Rather than trust my friendship with them, I let myself believe what he was telling the kids. Too many people were getting involved, and they demanded I show proof of Allen's drug use. I had lived with it long enough but had covered for him, so now it looked like I was the one with the problem, and everyone started taking his side.

Allen started sleeping in his truck, so Brad gave him his camper to stay in, saying he could keep a better eye on Allen that way. Then one day, Brad showed up at my house and told me that I needed to stop rebelling against the Lord and stay married, that he had been watching Allen and had seen no drug addiction. I told him I was continuing with it, so he then told me that I could no longer teach Sunday school. I asked if I was being kicked out of the church, but he said I wasn't, that the congregation just could not have someone who was rebellious to the Lord teaching Sunday school. I went in and got the lesson plans, and as I handed them to Brad, I told him Allen would make an ass out of him soon enough. The kids were watching from the window. This action only confirmed for them that I was in the wrong, and it isolated me from them even more. The older boys thought I needed to quit the church, but I told them I could not walk away until the Lord released me. So I continued attending service, though the seniors' wives would not even acknowledge me. Walking into the church that used to be so loving and have the congregation ignore me was one of the hardest things I had ever experienced, but I was there for my relationship with the Lord and not for these people who were taking sides. I was treated so horribly one Sunday at church that I started crying uncontrollably and left before service was over, and one of the ladies from the church followed me out to the truck. The lady gave me some scriptures and told me that more people than I realized were behind me and supported me. It gave me such peace to hear this and the strength to go on.

Allen still did not believe I was going through with the divorce and came over one day to fix the kitchen floor. He went to hug me as he was leaving, and I could smell the alcohol on his breath. Then he asked me to come out to the truck, that he needed to talk. I followed him out, and he asked me to go on a date. I could not believe he was serious and laughed at him.

Within a few months of Brad treating me so awful, he had a confrontation with Allen, where Allen had told him to get out of his house and mind his own business. John graduated high school, and on that same, weekend Broc was life-flighted in a helicopter because a bull had kicked him in the back at a high school rodeo. I was learning to trust the Lord and walk with Him and knew I was doing what I was supposed to and He would protect me.

CHAPTER 14

EMOTIONAL BATTLE

Finally, be strong in the Lord and in his mighty power. Put on the full armor of God so that you can take your stand against the devil's schemes.
—Ephesians 6:10-11

I was exhausted from the whole battle and ready to just give up, and then on Sunday at church, the pastor anointed me with oil and prayed over me. I could hear God telling me to hang in there and trust Him. I continued with the treatments every three weeks and the flu symptoms that followed a few days afterward. After I had barely survived my parents' divorce, I swore I would never put my children in the middle of one, and here we were with them hurting so awful and me unable to help with the pain because I was the cause of it.

August was a month that turned out to be more than I could handle. I was going to give Allen every weekend so the kids would not be disrupted during the school week by bouncing back and forth, but the judge said no and gave me every other weekend with them. He also ordered Allen to pay some child support. John headed off to college, and I had no resources to help him. He would be on his own for this college thing, and the guilt was almost more than I could bear. Daisy and I were going toe-to-toe. She would question everything I did, and she didn't want me around her. Broc and I got some special time together watching movies and hanging out while the other three kids were gone. My doctor told me to just keep telling the kids I loved them and they would soon see the truth.

Then Shelby got married, and old jealousy raised its ugly head. My dad had been invited to both Aponi and my weddings to walk us each down the aisle but refused to be there for us, and here, I had to endure him walking Shelby down the aisle and then getting that father-daughter dance that I had so desperately needed to experience. I felt he had abandoned me a long time ago and felt so ashamed to be so jealous of Shelby.

At my six-month dental cleaning, the hygienist discovered a spot in my mouth and had to biopsy it. Thankfully, it came back as a benign freckle, but while I was waiting for the results, I had to deal with all the old fears of cancer returning. I was so overwhelmed that I actually hit my knees and begged God to take me home. Then I started having severe bouts of vertigo. I wanted to just give up, but it was not to be. I was learning how God would not let me down no matter what, and I could not believe how messy my life had become. I was just trying to hang on. I would do a monthly budget at the beginning of each month and get so upset that my income came nowhere near enough to cover my expenses; however, I would pray and trust the Lord, and at the end of each month, I would look back in amazement that we always had the food we needed and all the necessities.

Allen's lawyer petitioned all of my medical records to try to prove I was too disabled to care for my children, which was hypocritical because I obviously was not too disabled to care for him all of those years. Shortly after he petitioned, we settled out of court. I also learned that he had been dating most of the time through our divorce proceedings and that the lady he was seeing had her children taken from her because of drug abuse, and so she moved back to Texas.

Daisy started attending church with me, and our relationship started turning around. Joy and I started a women's morning Bible study weekly, and I continued doing my morning devotional and spending quiet time with the Lord. Life slowly started getting better. I found such peace in those morning devotionals and learned to meet with God before I started the day and found I could handle things better.

I decided I wanted off the pain meds, and so when the kids went to Allen's and John was home for Christmas, I quit cold turkey. I later discovered you do not come off pills without doctors weaning you off of them. My heart was racing, and I had to run through the house for ten minutes at a time to get rid of the feeling that my heart was going to explode. Then I had the chills. I pulled the mattress in by the fireplace, and John packed on the blankets. It was a very rough week before I started feeling a little better. Sometimes wounds run so deep that there is never a complete healing, and things seem so dark that you doubt the light will ever return. I have heard a saying: "If there is enough cracks, the light can get in, and the more cracks, the more light." I think God was letting me be cracked open so that His light could get in.

CHAPTER 15

HASHIMOTO'S THYROID DISEASE

For when I am weak, then I am strong.

—2 Corinthians 12:10b

The New Year came in with me sitting at home and bawling uncontrollably, and at midnight, I called Allen and asked if he wanted to work things out. I told him that this is not what I was aiming for when I filed for divorce. I had hoped he would check into rehab and we would still be a family. He agreed, so we decided we would get counseling from the pastor and take it slow and do it right. The kids came home the next day all excited, and we proceeded to see the pastor on Wednesday nights.

I was not feeling well enough to go into my treatment, so I postponed for a day. When I went in, I was still not up to speed, so the doctor had me see the nurse practitioner on duty and put me in a room to run extra fluids and potassium. The nurse ran blood work and discovered I was severely anemic on top of other things and placed a blood transfusion bracelet on me. I was told if I passed out, I needed a blood transfusion. I went back a week later for more results from the blood work and discovered I had Hashimoto's disease, which meant my thyroid was burning out. Even after I started medications for the thyroid, I spent almost the whole month with bouts of vomiting and diarrhea. My gastroenterologist had me get another colonoscopy and ERCP, but all came back with good news.

I was completely off the pain meds and only feeling slightly achy, but thankfully, the Zometa was helping my bone pain. I still needed to rest often during the day, and then I ended up in the ER with the doctors saying my pancreas was flaring up again. I couldn't even get off the couch, so my sister-in-law drove me to the ER. I could not eat anything without severe pain and had to start with the BRAT diet (banana, rice, apples, and toast). Because I couldn't leave the house, Joy brought the supplies to me. What a blessing I had with the people in my life.

One night in late February, I awoke with what I can best describe as the Holy Spirit right above me, and I heard Him say, "This is only going to hurt for a second." Then He pressed on me. I awoke the next morning, singing, "Lord of heaven and earth," and I had such a peaceful feeling.

March began with this real-life dream of God showing me that a relationship with Him is like climbing stairs. Before you start your relationship with Him, you run all around and sin. Then you take that first step, and your way becomes narrower. Jesus is the handrail that supports you all the way up, and after you climb a flight, you get to stop and take in where you're at. It was years later that I read about Jacob's ladder in the Bible and was so excited that what I was reading was so close to what I had experienced. The realization that we all continue to sin and the joy at learning the Lord will still love me even when I mess up was a hard lesson to learn, but I was starting to get it.

Broc got really sick, and when I took him to the doctor, the staff discovered he had mono to the point that his throat swelled almost shut and he could no longer even drink fluids to stay hydrated, so I had to take him to the clinic for IV fluids. His spleen was so swollen that we were told if anyone even bumped him, it could rupture and become life-threatening.

Reconciliation didn't go so well. Allen started making excuses that he had paid child support but the check had gotten lost in the mail. Then our pastor got sick, and we could not meet on Wednesdays. I felt something was going on but couldn't put my finger on it, and one Sunday in April, the kids came home from spending the weekend with him. They were crying about how they never got to see their dad. Rather than say something I would later regret, I went out to the shop. Shortly thereafter, Daisy came out and said she knew something, but her dad had made her promise not to tell. I said I knew he had a girlfriend, and Daisy started crying and said he was engaged to a lady named Kristin who was in the process of getting a divorce. It goes to show that you cannot open back up a door that the Lord has shut, and I knew then I had to move on.

Allen soon moved Kristin and her three kids into the little single-wide trailer he was living in, and our kids hurt because they didn't get to see their dad much and did not want to share him with Kristin. When I had filed for divorce, I had not thought clear to this point. Although being married to Allen was killing me, at least I still had my kids under my roof, so I could protect them. Now I had no control over them while at his house. Cody's school drawings of his family included Kristin, but he was leaving me completely out, which hurt deeply. I did not know how I was ever going to fix our relationship. If it wasn't for my pastor's counseling and my friends at Bible study, I would probably have just crawled into bed and given up.

Allen was really unstable at this point. He would sleep with Kristin one night and call me the next day to say he was still in love with me. I learned to pray and trust God to protect my children. It was the only way to find peace. In May, Allen told me that he needed to talk to me and that he would meet me at the sports complex while Cody rode his bike. He said that Kristin would not be around. So I showed up, and out of the blue, he asked if I wanted to get married. He said that he still loved me. He did this on Mother's Day, and he wrote me a note stating how he still loved me and missed me.

Cody and Daisy wished to be baptized, which was arranged for the end of May. Daisy started attending church with me regularly and helped with the nursery and Sunday school, which had been given back to me. Toward the end of May, John came home from college for the summer and worked for a construction company. After one of my Herceptin treatments in June, I got a massive headache, and my back hurt so bad I could not fall asleep until early morning. I had been riding bikes with Cody and trying to spend time with him, so I had to pray through the pain and just keep going and trusting God for strength.

Daisy started fighting with Kristin and Allen and did not wish to go to his house, so I promised my kids that my house would always be a safe haven for them to escape to and that I would not date or bring a man into the house until they were ready. On June 13, Allen tried to get back together with me again, and this time, I told him to stop disrespecting both Kristin and me. He had Kristin and her kids living with him, and he was trying to get back together with me.

I got called one time to meet Allen and Kristin at the ER and pick up the kids, and I finally confronted her about their drug problem. (I also felt she had a problem.) She informed me that she used to have a drug problem but not anymore and was currently clean and then admitted that Allen was struggling with his problem.

Hashimoto's Disease

Hashimoto's disease is a disorder that affects your thyroid, a small gland at the base of your neck below your Adam's apple. The thyroid gland is part of your endocrine system, which produces hormones that coordinate many of your body's activities.

In Hashimoto's disease, also known as chronic lymphocytic thyroiditis, your immune system attacks your thyroid gland. The resulting inflammation often leads to an underactive thyroid gland (hypothyroidism). Hashimoto's disease is the most common cause of hypothyroidism in the United States. It primarily affects middle-aged women but can also occur in men and women of any age as well as children.

CHAPTER 16

WHEN THE LORD SPEAKS

Your hands made me and formed me; give me understanding to learn your commands. May those who fear you rejoice when they see me, for I have put my hope in your word. I know, O Lord, that your laws are righteous, and in faithfulness you have afflicted me. May your unfailing love be my comfort, according to your promise to your servant. Let your compassion come to me that I may live, for your law is my delight. May the arrogant be put to shame for wronging me without cause; but I will meditate on your precepts. May those who fear you turn to me, those who understand your statutes. May my heart be blameless toward your decrees, that I may not be put to shame.
—Psalm 119:73-80

The year came in with a lot of changes. I drove John back to college in the midst of a snowstorm, and it took twelve and a half hours at the wheel driving fifteen to twenty miles per hour the whole way in a complete whiteout. I then received a bill from my disability saying their office had overpaid me all this time and I now owed them $20,000 and needed to have it paid by March. So now on top of everything, I would be losing the amount every month that I had budgeted for. Broc was finishing up his senior year of high school, and Allen married Kristin on Valentine's Day.

I was still fighting unexplained vertigo off and on. My skin was really pale, and I had sunken eyes, so the doctor put me on some meds to try to help. I was fighting going back on pain meds, but I hurt on a continuous basis. The doctor ordered a brain scan because of all the vertigo, but it came back clean. In the back of my mind was the thought that I really was running out of time with my children.

Cody was really struggling with school, so I took him out and homeschooled him for the remainder of the third grade, thinking that the time together would help strengthen our relationship. Allen and Kristin moved to a hotel in Boise, and he told the kids that a white spot in his mouth was cancer, even though he had not been to the doctor. Because of my history with cancer, they were freaked out. Cody started fighting me on homeschooling, and he was lashing out at both Allen and me over the living arrangements.

Cody and I went on a bike ride, and he crashed his bike and slid his face across the sidewalk. I panic whenever I see blood on my children's face, and he had this gash across his chin with blood pouring out. I was trying to stay calm while the owner of the house we were in front of let us use her phone to call Broc to come and get us. I had to take Cody to the ER, where he received seven stitches in his chin. Broc was able to graduate, which made me very happy because he was the son I worried about the most when it came to making it through school. I would catch him fishing on school days instead of being in the classroom, so I was ecstatic when he got his diploma. John planned on spending the summer working at college, and Broc was moving out, so now it would be just me and the two kids. I went from a full house of six down to sometimes just myself in a few short years, and I was having a hard time adjusting while I was fighting bouts of depression and loneliness.

Allen was still at the hotel, so I had to let the kids go and stay with him. I prayed they would be safe. I wasn't feeling well as it was, and I kept having emotional breakdowns because the pain was so out of control. The doctor put me on Celebrex to try to help and then ran some other tests because I had a lot of pain in the liver area and severe diarrhea. On top of everything else in my life, I thought the cancer had spread and I was at the end. The MRI all came back clean. I had a massive headache along with it all, and the doctor thought I might need to see a counselor because I was so exhausted from stress.

Allen and Kristin moved back to our town but into a travel trailer in a park along with Kristin's three kids.

The end of July, Daisy came out of her bedroom while Cody was at Allen's and said she wanted to move and go to school with her cousins. I told her because I was on disability, we could live anywhere and was she sure she wanted to leave all her friends. She would be going into her sophomore year of high school. Daisy insisted she was positive, so I told her not to say anything to Cody until I could talk to him. I knew God wanted us to move when Cody came home later that same evening and shortly after walking in the door informed me he wanted to move north to go to school. I called Daisy out and accused her of talking to Cody, but they insisted they had not talked, let alone discussed moving. It was enough for me to know I needed to sell my house and head north to a much smaller town, possibly my hometown, depending on the housing availability. The kids and I decided to look at rentals in my hometown and surrounding areas at the end of July, and then I called a friend who was in real estate and put my house on the market. In a downed economy, I had people bidding on my house and a buyer within two days. We could not find a house for rent anywhere; however, there was a house for sale, and so we arranged to move in so the kids could go to school while I rented it until I could get the loan paperwork all worked out. I was promised over the phone a 6 percent rate, and so the payments would be possible. On August 25, I loaded the kids up and drove them to school in a small town thirty miles south of where I had grown up, less than a month from the day the kids told me they wanted to move. I then went and picked up the keys for my house. I would take the kids to school each day and drive down and get a load and work on cleaning the house and then pick the kids back up. All was going extremely smoothly until I went into sign the paperwork after I had rented for two months and found the interest rate was not what I had been promised but much higher. So my payments were much larger, but I had nowhere to move and felt I could not back out because the family I bought the house from was counting on me. I signed and figured I could make ends meet somehow.

Daisy was asked to the homecoming dance by Dirk. She was not doing much because she didn't play volleyball and basketball and because there was no dance team in the school. I started trying to get a cheerleading program up and running but ran into snags every which way. There were two schools in co-op for sports because the schools were so small and the one Daisy attended gave me the approval; however, I had to go through all the hoops of getting certified, and the other school still said no. So I would have to prove the program worthy to get the other school on board. I had only cheered my senior year in high school and coached basketball for young kids, so coaching cheer for teenagers was going to be an experience.

My treatments continued, but I had numbing feelings along the left side of my face. The doctor scheduled me for an MRI, and when it came back clean, he scheduled me for a lumbar puncture to check the spinal fluid. I drove myself home afterward, and by the time I got home, I had a major headache that took a few days to overcome. The spinal tap came back normal with no known cause for the numbing sensations. Daisy was really helpful during this time and took care of me while I struggled with a splitting headache for days afterward. Our first Christmas in our new town, Daisy and I went to the mountains and chopped down our own tree. It was snowing when we left for the mountains, and once we found the tree, we took turns chopping and laying on the tree to get better angles for chopping. It was a very wonderful experience, although our tree ended up being no taller than us at five feet. The two of us hadn't laughed that hard in a very long time.

CHAPTER 17

FORGIVENESS

Before I was afflicted I went astray, but now I obey your word.
—Psalm 119:67

It was good for me to be afflicted so that I might learn your decrees.
—Psalm 119:71

I was struggling with so much pain in the tailbone area that I could hardly walk. My body would just tremble from the pain, and so I would sleep with a heating pad. I would have to lie down often throughout the day.

After I got all the certified work done, I was approved to start up a cheer program as the head coach, and I planned my first tryouts for the month of April.

Aponi drove to my house, and we took Mom out dancing to celebrate her birthday. After we dropped Mom off and drove home, Aponi started crying, and we had time to ourselves to just talk. I didn't get many moments with my baby sis, and I tried to comfort her; however, I didn't know what to say. She was hurting so bad, the wounds running so deep and the scars so painful. I wanted to fix everything but couldn't get her to understand that God loved her and had already forgiven her. She was not forgiving herself or those who had hurt her, and it had festered so deep my heart just bled for her.

My grandma broke her hip and had to have surgery, so Mom asked me to go to the hospital to run interference between my aunt and Uncle Alvah. He blew up in the hall at my aunt, who left in fear of her life. I realized I didn't see him as that monster anymore, and he no longer had any hold on me. I got between him and his sister and stood my ground until my aunt got safely out of the hospital and then went back in to check on grandma. He came into grandma's room and looked at me blankly and asked who I was. He said he didn't recognize me.

In March, I had trouble getting out of bed because the rainy weather made it feel as if I was being pushed to the ground. I felt as if the weight of the world was on my shoulders . . . literally.

In April, I felt the need and wrote Uncle Alvah a forgiveness letter, even though he had never acknowledged what he had done to me. I realized that by forgiving him, I could move on with my life and that he didn't even remember who I was, so what he did didn't even faze him. It felt good to write that letter and move on. It was very healing.

I had to have CT scans and more MRIs, and this time, I had two new spots light up on my sciatica, meaning more new cancer lesions; however, the doctor didn't want to change my treatment program unless the pain became unbearable. There were no more options for treatments except to let it run its course. I constantly struggled with charley horses and hurting so much that I spent a great deal of time in bed. Allen and Kristin got tossed out of the trailer park and would be homeless, so Allen told the kids they were just going to spend the summer camping, and then they managed to move in with Kristin's daughter instead.

I was really struggling with bills, and I had anxiety attacks, so I took on a part-time waitressing job for a few days a week and for a few hours at a time to see if I could hold up.

I realized how hard it was to make the high house payments and started receiving threats that the house would go into foreclosure. I was stressing so much that I started getting sores in my mouth. I went to treatment and was in so much pain I started crying, and so the Oncologist insisted I needed to go back on pain meds.

My basement flooded with sewage a day before I had to leave with the cheerleaders to camp. The plumbers that fixed the problem informed me tree roots had invaded the pipes and it would only get worse.

I was able to switch my treatments to a closer facility so that I would not have to drive as far. I had completely lost my appetite, and I had to get another CT scan.

Now my truck started falling apart and needed work and new tires. I was sinking into despair, not knowing how much longer I could hang on to everything. Then while at work one day and my mom living next door, something happened to Mom's bathroom door, and she blamed Cody out of all the boys in the house and told him he was not welcome in her house. He was too scared to even go home to our house, which I had told him he would always be safe in. He denied putting the hole in the door, and I backed him, which meant another fight with my mother and whatever siblings she called and complained to. That meant phone calls from Aponi, Sunny, and Faith, although Faith never brought it up and said she was just checking on me. It is funny how I never heard from them unless my mom and I had problems. Then Mom kept putting notes in my truck saying that I needed to discipline my kids and make them apologize to her. What she didn't grasp was that I was the only stable person in my kids' lives and I had to stand by them or they would be completely lost.

The house flooded with sewage again, and it was too cold to open windows and doors to air out the place. It took the plumbers three days to fix the problem, and I discovered that my house has the lowest level basement in the area. So when the city manholes clogged, I got the backflow, and I was really sickened at that revelation.

I dropped John off at the airport at 6:00 a.m. for Christmas vacation and then went to pick up Cody at his dad's house. When I knocked on the door, it swung silently open, and I saw Allen asleep on the couch. I stood on the doorstep and kept calling to him, asking where Cody was, and he rolled over and sluggishly said Cody was asleep on the floor. Not seeing Cody, I asked where, and he said right there. Panic overcame me because the door hadn't been latched and Cody wasn't where Allen said he was, so by then, I was almost hysterical. I was shouting at Allen when Kristin came out of the bedroom and told me Cody was in the other bedroom and that Allen had been out of it all weekend on a binge. I left there, and I didn't want my son to ever go back, Allen in such bad shape and knowing drugs were the problem. I feared for my son's life.

I then had to have another colonoscopy, and so Daisy drove me this time. I dropped her off at her uncle's, and after I pulled over to vomit, I drove myself home. I knew I was not supposed to drive after surgery; however, I needed to get home, and this seemed the only way to do it.

CHAPTER 18

DEFLATED

This is the day the Lord has made; we will rejoice and be glad in it.
—Psalm 118:24

I took on coaching Cody's fifth—and sixth-grade basketball, but some girls were complaining that there was no basketball for them, so I formed a girls' team as well. Now I was coaching high school cheer and both boys and girls basketball.

I had to wake up every three hours to stoke the fire all through the night. It was 18 degrees below zero in January, and it felt like the wind was just howling through the house. We were getting so much snow I could barely keep it shoveled away from the windows, but thankfully, the wonderful people in the community were plowing out my driveway. I was shoveling and then lying on a heating pad intermittently, gritting my teeth to the pain.

March came and along with it more basement flooding, and then I went to the dentist and found out I needed to have a tooth pulled; however, because of the Zometa I was taking by infusion for my bones, there had been a side effect called osteonecrosis, deterioration of the jawbone. The dentist decided to just monitor as long as possible until more information came out about the side effects. My pain got the best of me, and I hurt so badly that I became bedridden. Daisy took care of me for a few days.

April arrived. I had more headaches, light-headedness, heart palpitations, and fatigue, and I was cold all the time. I got out of bed one morning, and just as my feet hit the floor, I blacked out and hit my head on the dresser. I later asked Daisy why she hadn't come to check on me, and she said she heard the crash but assumed all was okay.

Cody came home from school, and when I told him to do his homework, he grabbed his bike and started to go riding, so I grounded him. Cody then grabbed his phone and headed outside to call his dad to complain about me grounding him from his bike, and I told him to get back inside and took the phone. I took the phone, thinking I was going to get support on Cody doing his homework, but instead, Allen started calling me a fucking whore and other names, just screaming at me over and over. He said I had whored it up with an old man to get my truck fixed and that the kids say I just lay around all day, whining about my cancer. I was so blown away by the lack of respect from everyone that all I could do was lock myself in the bathroom, crawl into the bathtub, and sob. I decided at that point that the kids would be going and staying with him all summer because they needed to see how he lived and I honestly didn't know how much more I could take.

Sometime in May at 2:30 a.m., I got a text asking for the kids social security numbers I texted back that this fucking whore wasn't his secretary, and he texted back that I needed to show some class. I couldn't help but chuckle at that comment. After all, what kind of class does it take to text someone at 2:30 in the morning?

I ended up subbing all but a few days of the entire quarter, and in the last week, I woke up with my right implant deflated. After I called the doctor, I discovered he was booked for two weeks, so I was back to baggy shirts and stuffing my bra.

I then drove to Texas for Lilly's high school graduation and took Mom, Saffron, my niece, and Toby, my nephew, along. We drove the twenty-four hours straight through, and had we not gotten held up in a road construction, we would have arrived right in the middle of a tornado. The dawn showed us driving straight into blackness, and the radio wasn't working; however, then we were held up in the construction, and as we arrived at the destination, we could see cars still flooded in fields. I was so thankful the Lord was watching over our trip. Just a few days after Lilly's graduation, we loaded up to head back to Idaho, and as I hugged Aponi and Faith, I started crying. I hadn't realized till that point how much I missed my sisters.

Daisy flew with Dirk to Hawaii, and so Mom drove me to the surgery. It was supposed to be only one hour to replace both implants, but there was so much scar tissue that it turned into two and half hours. I was sent home with orders not to do anything for the first few weeks. My mom dropped me off, and I spent all my time home alone on the couch. I couldn't mow the lawn or do anything physical, and then just as I started to recover, I had to have the tooth pulled. I had been told that the bone could not be disturbed because of the Zometa. The dentist took his time to miss the bone, but in the end, he had to chip a little bit. I was sent home with meds, and again, I lay around to recover. With all the medical situations going on and running to and from doctors and surgeries, I fell behind with a house payment, which became the start to a two-year battle to save my home. If only I could have seen how this situation was going to turn out in the end.

Cody called after he had been at his dad's for three weeks and said he was homesick and wanted to come home, so I went and got him, and we spent the day driving around some back roads and visiting. I called my dad on Father's Day, but he kept trying to complain about my brother. I told him I would have to hang up if he continued because I loved them both and would not be forced to take sides between the two. It was the last good phone conversation we were to have. Cody stayed a few days, and then I took him back; however, he wasn't there long before he called one night, crying about him and Kristin clashing and him wanting to come home. I told him to sleep on it and that I would call him in the morning. When I called, he said he would stick it out. This was what I had been hoping for, namely he would appreciate all I did for him, but it still pained me for him to have to experience that hardship.

121

My jaw swelled up from an infection caused by the tooth extraction, and then in the beginning of July, I noticed my collarbone looked swollen. So I went to the doctor, and he did some more scans that showed all was okay except for some minor lymphedema; however, he figured the infection of my jaw had drained into that area, so I was put on antibiotics.

I went ATVing all over the mountains with some old friends, but by the time I got home, I was hurting so badly that I woke up the next day vomiting and hurting. I had to get ready to waitress anyways. I couldn't get Cody off my mind, and so I prayed continuously while he was at his father's. Daisy was upset with how bad her dad looked when she stayed there. She said that she didn't think he was going to last much longer, that he was missing another tooth and shook continuously.

Osteonecrosis

Zometa (zoledronate) is a bisphosphonate medication used to treat cancer patients. It is taken intravenously (through an IV).

The use of bisphosphonate medications, such as Zometa, Aredia, and Fosamax, have been linked to an increased occurrence of osteonecrosis of the jaw, a painful and potentially disfiguring jawbone condition. It is an irreversible condition in which the patient's jawbone decays and dies.

Lymphedema

Lymphedema is caused by a blockage in your lymphatic system, an important part of your immune and circulatory systems. The blockage prevents lymph fluid from draining well, and as the fluid builds up, the swelling continues. Lymphedema is most commonly caused by the removal of or damage to your lymph nodes as a part of cancer treatment. There's no cure for lymphedema, but it can be controlled.

CHAPTER 19

GOOD-BYES

A cheerful heart is good medicine, but a crushed spirit dries up the bones.

—Proverbs 17:22

Aponi called and said she was trying to look to God and that a lady friend and co-worker had been ministering to her and trying to get her to go to church. Cody called and said Allen was hauled off in an ambulance to the ER for heart problems. Two days later, the first weekend of August, I got a call from Allen at 9:00 a.m. to tell me Kristin had passed because of complications with her sleep apnea. My mind was reeling. Cody had been there and had witnessed the emergency crews trying to revive her. Allen said Cody was okay, and I couldn't get to them until the next day because I had no money for gas and needed to waitress first to get enough in tips. Upon arrival to the apartment, Allen showed me and Daisy that he had two boxes packed. He informed us he was getting rid of the rest of the belongings as soon as possible. He changed his story about how Kristin had died multiple times, and against my better judgment, I left Cody with him so that Allen wouldn't do anything stupid.

His stories ranged from a lithium overdose do to the fact she was disoriented most of the time so he took her prescriptions away from her and dosed them out morning and evening. Then he told us that she had forgotten she had taken them that evening and took them again so he said it was from overdose of her prescriptions. Over the phone the night before, Cody told me that he had been upset with Kristin when she went to bed and he would never be able to make it right now, but Allen sat there and tried to tell us that he and Cody had been joking with Kristin right before she went to bed. They said she had been falling asleep during her supper, so they told her to go to bed, which she did. He went on to tell us that at 4:30 a.m., her breathing machine was making funny noises, so he went in to fix the mask that had slid off sideways and put it back on. He said that she had looked up at him with a glazed look but didn't say anything. He said that Cody wanted to take a shower at 6:00, and so he used a flashlight to go into the bathroom for a towel, and when he shone it on Kristin, her lips were black. He called 911 and started CPR. Allen said Cody had seen it all, but Cody told me he had been in the bathroom. Something else that bothered me with this story was that Cody had never gotten up before 10:00 a.m. to take a shower on any day that wasn't a school day, so why would he be up at six o'clock and wanting a shower on a summer day?

I left Cody there but checked in often. I knew that caring people of the community were stopping in and checking on them, and I called often. On Monday, Allen told me he couldn't deal with the funeral home, so he signed a release for Kristin's dad to pick up her ashes for the funeral on Tuesday. He led me to believe there had been a funeral with Kristin's ashes and everything. Then on Wednesday, he said he had to get up early and go to the coroner's office and get the death certificate. Thursday morning, he told me he was struggling with the coroner over getting the death certificate, and then on Thursday night, he said that social security had contacted him and that their office must have automatically gotten the death certificate and that he was supposed to get a lump-sum. Then the conversation turned to the fact that a week before Kristin died, she received her social security letter stating what benefits would be available should she pass. He said he had thrown it away but had later dug it back out. This revelation gave me chills up the back of my neck.

I then had cheer camp and my nephew's wedding in Montana to attend. While I was in Montana, Allen called and said he was struggling with the funeral home because the manager wouldn't cremate the body and needed me to come get Cody so that the man could get things wrapped up and taken care of. On Saturday, I drove down and brought Cody home. I tried to just listen while he talked and he mentioned that Kristin had gone to sleep that night because she was tired because she had taken an Ativan or Xanax.

When I got home, I had a phone message from a sergeant with the Boise Police Department. He needed to talk to me about a case he was working on. I returned the call, and he informed me that the department was waiting for Kristin's toxicology report before they could rule her death and that the body was still at the coroner's. He also came right out and asked if I thought Allen could be responsible. Although I had my suspicions, all I could think to say was that he was the father of my kids and that I would like to hope he wasn't capable of such acts. The sergeant informed me that because of Allen's lifestyle choices, his mind was not all there and that I should not allow Cody to go around Allen's house anymore. I told him I would do my best to keep my son away. He told me that if I had to send Cody for a visit, then I should call the police and that the department would do a child check for me.

One day, we all received odd letters from Allen apologizing for all he had ever done, and then that evening, he told Cody that he was feeling odd and that Kristin had felt odd right before she went to bed, which caused Cody to distress. I called the Boise Police to check and asked that the officers check on Allen.

Rolling into September, Daisy started getting sick in the morning, and then one day during homecoming week of her senior year, I had another dreamlike trance. I saw Daisy and Dirk as homecoming king and queen, him in his football uniform, her in the cheerleading uniform, and then I saw a little girl about four years old sitting on my bed, telling me a story that had me laughing. The little girl would push the hair out of her face with her palm. It was so real that I called the school and ordered a bouquet of flowers for homecoming night that said congratulations, and then Daisy came home that day and informed me that Dirk and she were the senior homecoming candidates. On the day of homecoming during the pep assembly, Allen called to say his dad had passed away. I told him not to say anything to the kids so that Daisy could enjoy her last real school memory because I knew she was pregnant. At the game that evening when the staff crowned Daisy and Dirk homecoming king and queen with Dirk's mom taking their picture, it was exactly what I had seen in my dream.

I had to have another CT scan of my collarbone because the fluid still remained, but the scans all came back clean, except I had some lymphedema and needed some massage to work the fluid out. It turned out that Daisy was pregnant after all, and we found her a doctor in Boise. Daisy stayed in school, and although she could not cheer anymore, she went to practices and helped me coach the girls.

Aponi called near the end of September to talk about accepting Jesus and how things were going for her. It was a really nice visit, but she called me a few weeks later and said she was going to the doctor because of a pain she was suffering in her upper left side and that she needed me to pray for her. I felt so close to a melt down with all the finance problems, running Daisy to the doctors, and finding out she was so dehydrated that she almost needed to be hospitalized, and then Cody cried himself to sleep because I wouldn't let Allen get him. I hated having to be the mean parent to protect my child, Cody resenting me because of it.

Just when I couldn't take anymore, I got an e-mail from my long-lost friend, Merry. She had been my roommate in Japan and had helped deliver John. She was the friend I had lost because Dwayne had said that she was lying about him cheating on me. I am so thankful that true friendship never ends. I tried to limit my pain pills to one a week on Sunday after I waitressed a hectic weekend, but I noticed that a day after I took one a lot of blood showed when I blew my nose. I wasn't sure if the pain meds or the overexertion of waitressing caused the blood.

The beginning of November, I let Cody go visit his dad for the first time since Kristin's passing against everything I was feeling. Then

Allen called and said he wasn't bringing Cody home on Sunday night as we had planned but would just take him to school on Monday morning. Cody later told me that Allen had showed him an urn and said Kristin's ashes were in it and that Allen would just sit there and talk to her.

I was having a lot of vertigo episodes lately. It seemed to always happen in November. The week of Thanksgiving, I was going to let Cody go visit Allen after dinner on Thursday, but on Wednesday, his landlady called me and said she was trying to kick him out. She informed me that rent had not been paid for at least six months, and she said he had not worked for over a year, that Kristin had been the one working and supporting the family. Allen had told his landlady that he had Cody on the weekends and gave her a sob story about needing a place for Cody to come and visit. The lady told me she felt bad about kicking him out on Thanksgiving but that he had taken advantage long enough, so she was turning his power off that day. Allen didn't know I had talked to his landlady and tried to convince me he had power and Cody would be safe. He tried to say he was moving out that weekend after Cody went back home. When I confronted him about lying and told him that I had already talked to his landlady, he got agitated, but I stood my ground and did not let Cody go.

In December, I had one of my treatments. I was exhausted from running around all day, and then I was served papers stating the mortgage company was not going to work with me on a modification after all and was starting foreclosure proceedings. I had a complete meltdown.

I decided to throw Mom a surprise seventieth birthday party and started the planning phase and also spent the month struggling with migraines and nausea. I still had to climb on the game buses with a busy basketball schedule for the cheerleaders. The mortgage company decided if I would get a payment to their office, their team would work with me, so I needed to decide if owning this home was a pride thing. I made the decision that I was not going to lose anymore sleep over it.

Winter was just getting started, and I was already running low on chopped wood. Having to chop it myself also made me realize this house was more work than I was capable of providing. Allen got arrested for driving violations. The only brightness to all I was enduring was enjoying watching Daisy become a mother and getting to feel her baby kick. I had a headache and nausea on New Year's, and then I was going to run to Moscow to bring John home. He was snowed in and had to spend Christmas away but got the go-ahead to student teach at our school that semester, so he was moving home.

Chapter 20

A FULL HOUSE

I can do everything through Him who gives me strength.
—Philippians 4:13

John got to go to our school for his student teaching, and so I had four of us living in a two-bedroom house. I went to my six-month dental appointment only to discover my jaw had never healed, so the dentist had to open the wound back up, scrape out the scar tissue, pack it full of antibiotics, and start me on a stronger oral antibiotic. Then one day while I was doing dishes, I stuck my hand in a glass and a piece popped out and cut my thumb deep. I had to run and get stitches and then catch the bus to a basketball game. My body was taking a beating.

Now that I had been diagnosed with osteonecrosis (deterioration of the jaw), I would have to discontinue the Zometa treatment, which had also been keeping the pain under control and giving me strength. My thumb didn't heal completely either, so I had to take an antibiotic for that as well.

Aponi had been on my mind a lot lately, so I had been praying for protection and guidance for her.

My jawbone became infected again, and I hurt a lot more lately than usual. I was trying to just be at peace with everything going on—John's college graduation, Daisy's high school graduation, her baby, praying Daisy would graduate before she went into labor.

May came with graduations, John from college and then Dirk and Daisy from high school. Dirk signed up for the US Army National Guard so that he could care for Daisy and their baby. I got a letter stating that I qualified for the Obama home modification, and it stated that all I had to do was make three on-time payments and send in all the required paperwork and that then I would get the modification to save my home.

Two weeks after graduation, we went in for the doctor to start Daisy's labor. We spent the night before at a hotel and arrived bright and early. Because of complications with the baby's head being too large, Daisy's blood pressure shot up, and baby's heart rate disappeared on the monitors. The nurse pushed a button on the wall, and the room immediately swarmed with people running and throwing lines over their shoulder, and down the hall they went. I ran with them and told Daisy that Jesus was walking with her and to trust the Lord. I kissed her and ran back to the room, where Dirk's mom was getting him into his scrubs. I didn't realize I had been holding my breath until I got back into the room and gasped for air and started crying. She hugged me, and then we got Dirk down the hall, where he waited until the doctors stabilized Daisy and the baby. Then they let him go in to watch the delivery of their baby by emergency C-section. Dirk's mom and I waited out in the waiting room until a nurse came to tell us what was going to happen, and shortly after, we were notified that everyone was okay and that Dirk was in with the baby and Daisy would be out of surgery in a bit. Turns out that she had pushed the baby down so much that the doctors had to suction her back up and out for the C-section. I was so thankful for God's amazing grace and a healthy first grandbaby.

Dirk would be leaving for boot camp when his daughter would be two months old. he moved in with us so that he could get the full experience of being a dad, and now I had six people living in my two-bedroom house. I didn't wish to be one of those mothers who pushed her daughter aside and took over the raising of her grandchild, so I told Dirk and Daisy that I would stay out of their way but that I would sleep with my phone next to the bed in case they needed help during the night. There was only one night I was needed. and I was so impressed with how well those two worked together to take care of their baby.

Even though Allen had no driver's license, he had a vehicle and had been taking Cody camping in the mountains, and I discovered he had been kicked out of his basement and was now living out of his vehicle.

I was struggling with guilt for being on disability and was considering going to school or something. Then I researched my illnesses only to realize I was in a 1 percentile that was still alive. I was trying to live as if my cancer was in remission, not understanding that the lesions were throughout my spine and massively throughout the pelvic area in the bone. Plus, the treatment I went to every three weeks for the rest of my life was keeping the cancer from growing—except for the two new spots in 2007, nothing had changed. The scar tissue had balled up so bad on my left chest and back, and I was constantly trying to exercise to loosen it up.

July came, and Allen arrived to take Cody camping in the mountains; however, I found out they went to the city and then on down to some of Allen's friends' places for the weekend. Knowing the shape he was in and that he was driving with no license, I was infuriated that I didn't know where my son was for the weekend, and I made a promise to myself not to let Cody leave the area with him again. I had to protect my baby at all costs.

My jaw really started to hurt, and when I went for a doctor's appointment, we discovered my thyroid blood work was off and that we needed to adjust my meds. I also discovered the doctor was knowledgeable about a study that Duke University was doing on osteonecrosis and hyperbaric treatments, so I called for information.

CHAPTER 21

OSTEONECROSIS

Give the people these instructions, too, so that no one may be open to blame. If anyone does not provide for his relatives, and especially for his immediate family, he has denied the faith and is worse than an unbeliever.
—1 Timothy 5:7-8

Dirk left for boot camp, so my daughter would be a single parent for a while. They discovered I had gotten osteonecrosis of the lower jaw from my Zometa treatment, and because the doctor quit administering it to me, I noticed that the pain in my bones was increasing, so I had to go on pain pills again. I then had to go to a cutting-edge treatment called hyperbaric for the osteonecrosis and had to do forty treatments or dives, as doctors referred to them because of the pressure of oxygen forced into the chamber I was sealed up in. I couldn't wear makeup or contacts or put anything in my hair during this time. I also had cheer going on and had to meet the bus and go to games after treatments. On some days, I was going to hyperbaric and then over to my Herceptin treatments and then racing off to a volleyball game somewhere. In September at one of my treatments, I had a poor blood return from my port and was so fatigued I could barely function.

I had hyperbaric one day and then needed to bide my time until a volleyball game, so I thought I would go to Veterans Park in Boise for lunch and relax. I found a nice little remote area with a table under a tree and sat down, but shortly after that, I heard this man shouting and talking to himself and heading straight for me. I really got nervous but continued what I was doing when he stopped just a few feet from me and then kept moving so that he was at my back. I told him he was making me nervous and to please not stand there. He apologized but continued talking to himself out loud about me. I got my phone out just in case and started praying. Then another man walked up to him, and I could hear them arguing over me, saying that the first man had seen me first. I packed up my things and took off as they hollered at me to come back. I decided I would never stop by myself at a park again.

The mortgage company sent me a letter saying that I had to follow the modification rules for another three months because they were still working on the paperwork. Dirk wanted Daisy and the baby to fly down to his graduation from boot camp. His mom was living in Texas by now, and I was pretty sure she was using all of Dirk's paychecks.

Dirk's mom said she had all the reservations made for Daisy and the baby to travel by air to Texas and meet up with her and then rent a car and drive to North Carolina. Then they would take Dirk after his graduation to Alabama for his ATI.

I was so stressed on the day I put my daughter and four-month-old grandbaby on the plane for Texas, and then I had to go to girls' volleyball districts. I was trying to keep everything in perspective, but my fear for my daughter's safety was overwhelming.

Daisy called me the next morning and told me she had no idea where she was. She did not go to Dirk's mom's friend's house as planned and she was at Dirk's great-grandmothers instead. Dirk's mom had a man with her she had met on the Internet and only met in person a few days prior to Daisy's arrival. They had taken her from the airport at night while she and the baby were in the backseat of the car, so she had no idea where she was and told me she was scared.

When they got ready to drive to Carolina, Daisy texted me and told me that Dirk's mom's boyfriend was going on the road trip and to pray for her. I got on MapQuest to see the route they should take and told her to text every hour through the night so that I knew where they were should something happen. I spent the whole night praying. It was a very traumatic experience for the two, one that would have lasting consequences. Dirk's grandfather flew in from Hawaii to take over, and after they dropped Dirk off at his ATI in Alabama, they drove back to Texas and dropped off Dirk's mom and her boyfriend. Then after he discovered that Daisy only had a one-way ticket, his grandpa put her and baby on a plane home. I had never been so relieved to see them.

Over Christmas break, Dirk proposed to Daisy. They set the date for June 2010. Then Dirk had to go back to ATI for two more weeks before he returned home permanently. While all this was going on with Daisy, I once again had water backing up in the pipes and could not get anything to flush. The tree roots were getting even more problematic.

After being released from the county jail, Allen ended up in the Boise jail for a thirty-day sentence and then was moved into the Rescue Mission on a rehab program. A dear childhood friend of mine was diagnosed with pancreatic cancer, and we e-mailed a few times while he was going through chemo and radiation. He told me he loved me bigger than the sun. The winter had been a harsh one, and I was getting so sleep deprived because the woodstove would not hold a fire. I had to get up every two hours and stoke it to keep the house even tolerable. The house was becoming more of a curse than a blessing. With payments so high, I never had any finances to improve the living conditions, and I was learning to live one day at a time.

CHAPTER 22

BLESSINGS

The Lord will guide you always; he will satisfy your needs in a sun-scorched land and will strengthen your frame. You will be like a well-watered garden like a spring whose waters never fail.

—Isaiah 58:11

The year 2010 started out with the planning of my daughter's wedding. We had six months, and I knew I would be paying for the whole thing, so I started praying immediately. If Dirk was not God's plan for my daughter, I asked that He please put stumbling blocks in the way, and then I prayed for finances to cover the wedding. Because it would take place outdoors in June, I also prayed for beautiful weather. Now I just needed to walk in an attitude of belief that my prayers would be answered.

I was still waiting for my house to get the Obama modification, and I was constantly on the phone with the mortgage company. I had been making the promised payments on time every month, and the people just kept giving me three-month extensions.

Everywhere we went—picking out Daisy's dress or ordering the cake and all other wedding necessities—we were given a discount, or the cost was under the budgeted amount. No stumbling blocks were ever put in the way. When I took the cheerleaders to the girls' state and boys' district games over a weekend, I sat in the hot tub, and because my immune system was so messed up, I ended up with folliculitis. The doctors ran my thyroid and discovered the counts were off, and this time, I was being overdosed. They readjusted my meds, and as always, I continued my treatment at MSTI every three weeks.

After one of Cody's basketball games, he ended up getting sick from eating at a fast-food place and spent a few days so ill he slept on the bathroom floor, and then I ended up getting whatever it was because I had to clean up and care for him those few days. I dragged out a mattress and slept on the floor next to the bathroom for a few days, only able to sip on Gatorade. When I started to feel a little better, I walked out of the bathroom and walked into what appeared to be an invisible wall. I stumbled backward and regained my balance, and I heard God ask me why I would give Him my small illnesses but wouldn't hand over the cancer. I decided then and there I was going to live as if I had been healed, but that also brought other questions. If I believed I was healed, why would I continue to go to the doctor for treatments? The Lord would give me answers to these questions a few years later.

In the spring, my aunt was taken home to the Lord from her battle with cancer. I had stopped by her house to see her a week before and made sure she was at peace with the Lord, and then I prayed all the way home. A month later, I was notified my childhood friend was fighting for his life in the hospital from the pancreatic cancer and was not expected to make it through. I went to the hospital to say good-bye, not understanding why God takes home some of us and leaves others fighting with the same illnesses. It is something I will probably never know the answer to, and I have to fight the guilt of still being around. His funeral was one of the hardest I had been to, and because I was holding my breath when I went past the casket, I almost passed out. I was trying to keep from sobbing, but it ripped through the silence.

In April on the Thursday before Easter, I received in the mail a letter informing me that I did not get approved for the Obama modification. So I called Saxon Mortgage Company and asked what the next step would be, and I was informed that I could do nothing and that my house would sell the next morning. I started having a meltdown, but when I hit my knees and started to pray, a peace came over me that all would be okay and that when one door closes, another opens. I got up and trusted God with the whole situation. The next day, I called the mortgage company, and their office told me who had bought the house and how to contact them. Because it was Easter weekend, no one was in, so I had to wait until Monday morning. I called the company before the staff even had the information on their desk. Their paperwork showed that they had purchased an abandoned house, but they went on to explain how the process of taking over possession would work. They told me a real estate person would contact me, and that evening, sure enough, she was on my doorstep. I told her I would not give her any problems, but I asked her to please not post any signs or do anything that would embarrass me because I lived right on Main Street in such a small town. The lady asked how long I would need to get moved, and I told her I had to find a place and that I did not get paid until the end of the month, so I was given thirty days. She then gave me her card and told me if anyone showed up to take possession, that person needed to contact her. I had to sub at school the next day and found two house prospects to rent. I went home for lunch, and as I was eating, a truck pulled up outside with a trailer full of tools. The couple informed me that they were there to put a lock on the door and secure the property and that I needed to get out. While I was telling one of them that he needed to call the real estate agent, the other one was taking pictures of me, and it was all I could do to be civil. They called the name on the card and apologized. Then they got in their truck and left. Had I not gone home for lunch, the house would have been locked up tight with all my possessions inside.

I went back to the school to finish out my day, and after I prayed, I called the numbers for rentals. The first place Cody and I went to did not feel comfortable and started to send me into a downward spiral of despair. I clung to God's promise of taking care of us, and a few days later, when we were looking at the second house out in the country, I knew it was the one. When it is God's will, it is amazing how smoothly things flow. My sister told me about a thing called "cash for keys." The mortgage company will pay to get tenants out of the houses quicker, and I called the real estate agent, who contacted the lender and approved me. I then went to moving as fast as I could, and within a week, I was moved completely out. The cash paid for my utilities to be switched over and left me with a large sum of cash to finish paying on Daisy's wedding, which I had been struggling with. Satan throws things at us to knock us to our knees, but that puts us in the best position to start praying and trusting God. He blessed me with a beautiful log house out in the country, a house that was so peaceful with a sweet little landlady.

I learned to keep things in perspective, and when things like this came along, I learned to ask myself if it was life or death and if not, to let it go. My rent was a third of what my house payment was, so I was already feeling financial relief, and I would no longer have to deal with my basement flooding with sewage from pipes backing up. I was trying to move along with waitressing and cheer tryouts, and I was hurting so bad that my back and left leg kept locking up. The doctor was debating about having me go ahead and receive radiation on the two spots discovered in 2007, but I was able to deal with the pain. I got home and had to take five loads of laundry to the laundry mat because my dryer had broken in the move. My dad had called about the wedding invitation he received. I called him back, and the conversation didn't go so well. After a week like the one I was having, I just had enough. He was trying to pick a fight, and I told him he was invited and could show up if he wanted.

Broc signed on for the US Marines. I kept getting migraines so intense I would vomit, so I was scheduled for a CT scan of the brain and chest X-rays. Allen had planned on riding his bicycle all the way from Boise so that he could give our daughter away, and we had his brother, Marlon, prepared in case Allen wasn't available; however, I told the kids to tell him I would come and get him for the weekend and take him home. My dad couldn't drive to give me or Aponi away at our weddings, and here Daisy's dad was going to ride his bicycle for days to be there for her.

I could not believe how beautiful and peaceful it was at the rental house and how much I loved being out in the country again.

CHAPTER 23

NO PLAN B WITH THE LORD

But when you ask, you must believe and not doubt, because the one who doubts is like a wave of the sea, blown and tossed by the wind. That person should not expect to receive anything from the Lord.

—James 1:6-7

The week of Daisy's wedding, we started having severe rainstorms that were causing major flooding and road closures. Aponi flew in, and between her and Shelby, they convinced our dad to attend the wedding. I also had a cold and had to have treatment the week of the wedding. Two days before the wedding, people started calling and asking what plan B was because of the rain. I told them I had been praying, and no stumbling blocks had been put in the way, so I knew God would make it a beautiful day. With God, you don't need a plan B. I quoted James 1:6 about when you ask and believe, it will be given, and if people did not trust my faith, they could always bring umbrellas.

On Thursday, we drove to get Allen, Daisy's stepsister, and the tuxes. On Friday, I had to get the cheerleaders together for a bake sale, and it started to downpour just as they sold their last item. I then drove out to the ranch as the table and chairs were being delivered, and the river was flowing so high it was coming up over the road in areas. That night, we had my granddaughter's first birthday party and then the rehearsal. Allen was staying with us for the weekend.

The morning of the wedding, the sun came out beautifully, and everything went off magically as my baby girl got married. After we cleaned up after the reception and everyone left, the rain started back up, and flooding took place the next day.

In July when I went to treatment, the nurse noticed I had high blood pressure and a rapid heart rate, so she called my doctor's office. As I was headed home, the doctor's office called my cell to have me stop in, so I had to turn around and go back. The cause would not be diagnosed for another year.

Broc got called up to leave for US Marine boot camp the first of August. I had started going to get massages to loosen the scar tissue and help with the headaches. Later, I discovered Broc's graduation from boot camp would happen the same week Cody had no school for fall. We planned a road trip so that Cody could see the beach. At fourteen, he had never gotten to walk on the beach. My mom would be going as well, and because she had never been to Disneyland, we planned to stop by there. Then because we were driving, Daisy and my granddaughter decided to go along, and because I had never seen the Redwoods, I decided to go through Northern California.

Broc was to graduate boot camp the end of October, and so I started planning our trip. In September, I kept having really strong urges to pray for my sister, Aponi, and the Bible study group had a counselor on sexual abuse give a talk and share some handouts. So I thought I could minister to Aponi. I started collecting information on how to help my sister, and I planned when she came home the following July to sit with her and deal with this issue. After all these years, we needed to talk about what had happened and help each other to heal.

I had a dream that seemed so real I wanted to understand it but couldn't. There were two girls playing in a field of wheat, laughing and running from each other, one with golden hair and the other with dark hair, and they were almost the same age but not twins. I thought maybe it was Aponi and me when we were little but could not make sense of it. I started struggling with weakness and a severe sore throat but wasn't sure what was wrong. I had a hard day with frustrations over life and then went to my Bible study, where a gentleman of the Lord was speaking. Afterward, he came up to me and asked my name. He then went on to tell me that I would do great things for the Lord and be blessed with so much joy and that I just needed to leave the past behind. I started praying on the trip and which route to take, and before I knew it, the car was packed and ready to go with my mom, Cody, Daisy, and her daughter. Four generations spanning seventy years crammed into a car for a week-long road trip.

The first day, we stopped and had dinner with my cousin, Star, and her family, and then we arrived at Crescent City, California. At fourteen, Cody had never seen the ocean, and so the next morning in the middle of a storm, we set out to explore. I fell in love with the lighthouse and took pictures at the docks and then drove to the nearest beach, where the waves were smashing into the rocks.

That day, we drove through the Redwoods, across the Golden Gate Bridge, and into Oakland. The power was out in areas, and I missed our lane exit. It was dark and late, and we were tired, so I pulled into a desolate parking lot and looked at the map. After we decided that we would stay on this route and go down the coast and in the morning shoot over to Anaheim, I got back on the crazy road. The next exit was a connector to get back on our original route. I still cannot find this on the map, but within minutes, we were back on track and drove as far as we could before we stopped to spend the night.

The next day, we drove to Disneyland and met up with another cousin and her family and spent two days in Anaheim. Then we drove to Oceanside but decided to stop and say hi to the kids' great-uncle before we went to the beach. When we were getting ready to leave, Cody noticed the front tire was wore down and sitting at an angle. Their uncle was concerned, and I told him that God had gotten us there. We went ahead and loaded up for the beach, and I trusted God the car would be okay. Their uncle called before we even got to the beach and insisted we come back and leave the car with him while we go on down to Broc's graduation. He had a large SUV and insisted we take it.

After we played on the beach, we went back and switched vehicles and headed on to San Diego for the night. Broc had a family day pass, so we spent the day with him and then rested up at the hotel. The next day, we got to his graduation just as he was being dismissed, loaded up, and took Mom to the airport, where I walked her to the gate so she could fly to Texas. Then we headed back to their uncle's to switch out vehicles. He discovered that the axle was bent and that he had installed all new tires and fixed the windshield for us. No one could believe I had driven clear from Idaho with the car in that condition, and their uncle told me that when I said it wasn't me holding the wheel, I wasn't kidding. Shortly after I returned, I started feeling fatigued and got a chest cold. I had no energy to do anything and couldn't even work out with my cheerleaders. My voice would come and go, and it would take everything I had to climb out of bed.

Chapter 24

SET FREE

Time does not heal all wounds, only forgiveness will start you on the path of healing.

—Joyce Meyers

The year started with me continuing to feel extremely ill and fatigued, and the only one available to help my mother haul hay for her and her brother, Uncle Alvah. When we first started hauling, I could help load and unload two trucks. The beginning of February, I had CT scans that came back with no changes and then went to see my gastroenterologist, but because I arrived ten minutes late, I was sent home. I was so upset because I had driven for two hours, fighting bad roads and traffic and not feeling well at all, and my eyes were hurting with stabbing pain and redness, which the doctor thought was an infection and then later ulcer or allergies to the hay I was hauling. I was making weekly trips to the eye doctor to rule out each and get glasses ordered because I could no longer wear contacts.

On my trip in the bus to McCall with the basketball team, I had a missed call, and when I went to listen once I got cell service, I heard mom crying and saying my grandmother had passed away, so I called her upon arriving at the school. I had to help Mom and Uncle Alvah with the planning of the funeral. I had been able to come to terms with Uncle Alvah and all he had done to me and the family and forgiven him, and now I was gathering information so I could help Aponi when she came home to the family reunion in July. Mom set me up to take him shopping for pants. Here, I was standing outside a dressing room while my uncle was trying on pants. I had once wanted so desperately to kill this man and had hated him with every fiber of my being.

Because the CT scans were clear, my oncologist thought my fatigue was due to depression, so he put me on an antidepressant. I took it for only a week before I insisted that I was not depressed and refused to take the medicine. I felt severe pain and fatigue so much that I couldn't hold my head up at times. My symptoms kept changing though, so it was hard to pinpoint the exact problem. My right side was cramping so bad it would cause pain up my back and shoulder to the point I would find myself holding my breath and I would have to concentrate on breathing. My body felt as if it was shutting down on me. I would wake in the night, gasping for air as if I had quit breathing. My feet were swollen upon waking, and I had jerky motions that would wake me up. I would go to take an afternoon nap from the fatigue and wake up four hours or more later. The end of March, I ended up driving myself to the ER over an hour away and had Daisy meet me so she could take Cody back to the house. When I got out of the truck, my legs gave out, and I stumbled. I was in so much pain, and my upper abdominal cavity was engorged. After many tests, the ER doctor informed me I had bowels backed up and gave me a cleansing drink and sent me home. I argued that something else was going on, but he said to see my doctor then. I spent a day in April with another massive headache and vomiting as my right side continued cramping on a regular basis. When I finally got in to see the gastroenterologists, he told me in the first five minutes that the problem was my liver or gallbladder, and I was also informed I had a hernia on my left side; however, the ER results showed it had been there for some time. I was scheduled for an X-ray and ultrasound of my liver and gallbladder the following day. The results came back from the ultrasound and showed that my gallbladder looked like it had some sludge. I had to wait till I could get scheduled for an ERCP in June. I had been hurting for nearly six months now, and I was finally getting answers for all the new aches and pains. The eye specialist told me the eye problems were because my immune system was attacking them, same as my other illnesses.

In April after Daisy had sent out invitations to everyone and planned my granddaughter's birthday party, my mom scheduled a graduation dinner for Saffron a half hour before the time already set for the birthday party in a whole different town. My mom then proceeded to start trying to get Daisy to change the party date, saying it was Saffron's day and she came first. She posted a remark on Daisy's Facebook wall stating Saffron was more important, but Daisy refused to get upset and just told family to come if they could. Toward the end of the month, Saffron was running track at state, so Mom and I were going to drive down and watch, but the night before, Mom called me extremely intoxicated and started going on about how Saffron was first and Daisy needed to change the birthday party because she was ruining Saffron's day. The day of the meet, I woke up with a headache and didn't care to spend the day with my mom after what she had said the night before so called and canceled.

The next week, I was taking an afternoon nap when the house phone rang and my mom left a message. Cody came into the bedroom and told me I needed to call Grandma because she didn't sound very good. I told him I really didn't want to deal with anyone's death right now, thinking it was news about my uncle. My cell rang about that time, so I answered and could not understand my mom because she was bawling hysterically. She said Aponi had taken her life and was gone. I couldn't breathe. Trying to comprehend what she was saying, I asked her to repeat it slowly and then told her to just hang on, that I was headed that way. I hung up and collapsed onto my bed in shock, sobbing hysterically. Cody held me while I sobbed it out, but then we had to hastily get ready and head out the door. He drove while I called Faith to see what was going on. I was in shock and could not wrap my mind around the reality of it. As far as I had known, Aponi had been doing so wonderful, and she was happy. We arrived at my mom's, and then shortly afterward, Rose arrived. While we were talking, Cody drove down to Uncle Alvah's. Our conversation was about me thinking the phone call from mom was news about Uncle Alvah or Sunny, because of their health problems. Then my mom made a comment that blew me away and changed my life. She said that she would have been able to handle all this better had it been me instead. The room got deathly quiet. I just stared at her in disbelief as she looked me in the eye with a challenge as if to say, "Yes, I said it, and I mean it." Everything went into slow motion as I tried to understand how a mother, my mother, could say such a thing, but at the same time, there was such a lifting as if after all these years of trying to earn my parents' love, I was set free. I got up and went into the kitchen to catch my breath, and Mom changed the subject by telling me there was some diet Pepsi next to the refrigerator. I sat back down and continued in conversation, all the while wanting to escape, so as soon as Cody showed back up, I left after I said that there was no need for both me and Rose to be there.

I was willing to forgive my mom for the comment because I knew she was in shock and that Aponi had been her baby girl, but the next few months would become too much for me to handle. I came to find out that the police had called my dad that morning but that he never called any of us until that afternoon, and when he did call, it was to my sister-in-law. When I called him later that night, he started in about all the stuff he had given Aponi. It was at my mom's, and I needed to get it. I sat down and started writing the list, and after about the fourth item, I put the pen down and asked myself what I was doing. I just continued to listen, knowing I was done with my parents. I would always love them, but I needed desperately to separate myself from them.

I had spent the past year putting together a family reunion of my grandmother's siblings and all their descendants scheduled for July 2, and my sisters were all coming home from Texas. It would have been the first time Mom had gotten all six of the kids together since I had been a freshman in high school, and because my mom blamed me for the failed attempt the last time Faith was in town, I was excited to make it right; however, it would never happen now.

I went to work on Friday, the day after receiving the news, so that I wouldn't be home alone with my thoughts. I needed to stay busy. I did fine until one of Aponi's old boyfriends came into the restaurant. After he left, I told his employee to let him know. About ten minutes after he had left, he came rushing back, and I just started bawling while he held me. When I got off work, Cody and I packed up and headed down to Daisy's for the night so we could attend the birthday party and Saffron's graduation the next day.

The birthday party was the next day, and then we rushed to Saffron's graduation. My mom was cold toward me, so we didn't hang around long before we headed home. Sunday was a hard day, and I woke up bawling, unable to face the day, so I called into work and went back to bed till 3:00 p.m. My mom then called and told me she had planned a memorial for 2:00 p.m. at the family reunion on July 2 and that she had gotten the okay from Lilly and that we needed to get an obituary written and into the paper ASAP. I had scheduled the family reunion from ten to six, so I told her that would not work for multiple reasons; however, she insisted Lilly was okay with it. I called Faith, and she said that was not right, and then later at about 11:30 p.m., Lilly called and also told me she had said no. Lilly was hurting so badly, and I didn't know what to say to help her, so I told her I was always available for her to call. Then I stayed up till 2:00 a.m., unable to sleep in case she needed to call back.

I went to my mom's the next day to write the obituary, and Hope, Aponi's childhood friend, came over and asked me what park the memorial would be held at on July 2. She showed me that Mom was already going ahead with plans that no one wished for. On Tuesday, I got up and ran to MSTI for a massage to work on the scar tissue, especially in my back. Next, I had to run to get my mom's prescriptions and then waitress. I called Lilly when I got home to talk some more, and I didn't get to sleep until 1:00 a.m. I was running hard, so I wouldn't feel anything, and I had to turn around and waitress again from 10:00 a.m. to 3:30 p.m. I went to work again on Thursday at ten o'clock and checked in with Mom at 12:30 because she had gone to the doctor for a head trauma she had received from a jack coming loose. I got off at 1:30, ran out, and retrieved Mom to take her to the hospital for a CT scan.

We decided to have a memorial on the eighteenth, and then during the family reunion weekend, we would have one with all the family;

however, Lilly held us off on the obituary because she wanted to come home and plan the memorial. I was so frustrated by now with my mom because of the situation with the birthday party and Saffron's graduation and how she was bullying everyone with the memorial, still not understanding why she had said what she had. On Friday, as I was headed to work, I received a phone call from Lilly telling me all of us in Idaho just needs to back off and that she will take care of everything when she gets there. I wasn't sure why I was the one receiving the phone call, but when Lilly started crying, I told her to turn her phone off and quit answering, and when I called both parents to tell them to leave Lilly alone, they both denied bothering her.

CHAPTER 25

BROKENHEARTED

Though my father and mother forsake me, the Lord will receive me.
—Psalm 27:10

I worked Saturday night and then on Sunday morning, and I was hurting pretty bad by this time and could barely walk; however, the physical pain helped take the focus off the emotional pain. I then ran home and gathered up John and Cody and headed to Boise to Daisy's. I took John to the airport and then tried to relax before surgery the next day. Monday came around, and I went with Daisy to her ultrasound. It turned out she was seven weeks and a day with child. Broc flew in while I was in surgery for an ERCP to make sure my symptoms were not liver-related. The doctor said the studies showed that all subjects that had been diagnosed the same time as me had already had liver transplants. The surgeon informed me that the liver and bile ducts actually looked better than they had fifteen years ago, so the primary sclerosing cholangitis was still under control, and now we knew it was my gallbladder causing all the pain. Cody was to drive me home, and Daisy picked Broc up at the airport and then drove him to the hospital to meet up. I was so out of it after surgery that I posted on Facebook that all was well and then lay down. I woke up three hours later to my mom talking on the answer machine and discovered the boys were gone. I see she had called multiple times while I was asleep, so I returned the call only to be berated for not calling and telling her how the surgery had gone and posting my status on Facebook instead. The conversation ended with my mom hanging up on me. I felt like she was trying to control me, and because she wasn't getting her way, she was angry. She was hurting from the loss of Aponi and needed to focus all that anger on someone, so I had the target hung around my neck.

The doctor's office called and said my TSH, which was my thyroid test results, were at 7.2, and the doctors were calling in new prescription. Two weeks after my little sis's death I woke up bawling, my jaw hurting so badly from trying to hold back the tears and grimacing in my sleep. Then the tears turned to anger. I was angry at the whole world. I wanted to scream at my parents for the role they had played in Aponi's death and at Aponi herself for feeling so helpless, and worst of all, I was angry at myself. I should have been more tuned in to Aponi's pain and should have been there for her. We were best friends growing up and inseparable, so why did I not help my sister?

I was referred to the surgeon to plan my gallbladder removal and have the tests he needed. I continued to work and keep as busy as I could so I would just fall into bed, exhausted each night, unable to form a single thought. I was supposed to be in charge of a speaker for the memorial but held off contacting anyone as Lilly asked. Then my mom called to tell me that she had found one, and when I told her his beliefs were LDS, her reply was that it didn't matter because Aponi wasn't anything. I could have screamed at her because it did matter. Aponi had accepted Jesus and had called me on several occasions in the past few years to discuss my relationship with the Lord and her struggles. So when Lilly flew in, I told her the name of the speaker I had in mind and that Lilly had met him a year before at Daisy's wedding. Lilly called him, and he agreed to speak.

I went to Bible study, where the group prayed for me, and I realized how much love I felt in that room. When I was with my own parents, I felt nothing but pain and stress. My nephew arrived in town and had a bonfire at mom's house so that we could all get together. I stayed as long as I could, but being around mom after what she said was like throwing salt into a raw wound.

Faith called me when she landed and asked if she could spend the night and arrived at 11:00 p.m. We got up and finished the last few details of the memorial with Lilly. Mom called because she wanted to know the plans and when Faith was coming up, and we told her we would meet her at the school at 11:00 a.m. We took family pictures and had an amazing memorial to honor our sister. At one point. Mom was having trouble. I went to hug her, and she turned her back on me and walked off. She left me just standing there. Mom didn't even acknowledge me at the service, so I kept my distance. She had told Lilly that she wanted to sit between Lilly and Faith; however, Faith changed up those plans, and we sat in order of birth, leaving an empty chair to represent Aponi between Mark and myself. So Mom sat between Mark and Lilly. Because family all came home for the memorial, people could not come back for the reunion. I had told Faith that Mom had said something really hurtful, so Faith told me to just give it time and distance myself until things calmed down. I realized just how alone I felt in a room full of family, but when I was home alone with God, I never felt alone. There is no pain in being loved by the Lord, and the love that I had spent a lifetime searching for was the Lord's love. It overflows the heart.

I woke up one morning and checked my Facebook only to discover Mom had posted a note on Aponi's wall stating that she was still getting the cold shoulder from you-know-who and she was still waiting on the letter her and Aponi had been laughing about in their last conversation, which meant that Mom and Aponi had been making fun of me in their last phone conversation. That little post probably hit me harder than anything Mom had done so far. To think that my little sister didn't know I loved her and was making fun of me hurt to the core, and the fact that Mom was rubbing it in was toxic to my soul.

I had to go meet my surgeon to go over the results of the HIDA scan and plan my gallbladder surgery. It turned out my gallbladder was 97 percent functional, which meant it was squeezing down 97 percent, which was why I felt the cramping and pain in my right side and up through the shoulder. The surgeon wanted to make sure the pain was not caused by cancer in my rib cage, so we scheduled an MRI for the following morning. I spent the night with Daisy and checked my Facebook only to see Mom had posted how she would trade places with me if she could, so I deleted it. After what she had posted that morning, I felt that this comment didn't ring true and that she was putting on a show to make it look like she cared.

On July 2, I got to the park and set up for the family reunion at ten o'clock, and everyone started arriving shortly thereafter. It was a great turnout, and I sent my son with my cousin to go camping. I would pick him up on the Fourth of July. I awoke on the Fourth of July with such a headache I could hardly think and felt extremely swollen even in the face, but I drove up to get Cody and take him to the bike park for a bit before I headed home. I was so fatigued at the bike park that I slept in the car the whole time Cody rode.

The next day, I got ready and headed to the massage I had scheduled before my treatment. The masseuse noted I was swollen, and so she worked on the lymph system to get some drainage. Then at my treatment while the nurse was taking my vitals, she discovered my heart rate was at fifty beats per minute, and so I was asked what my MUGA scan showed. I had never had my heart checked, so I did not know what a MUGA scan was. The doctors informed me that I needed a scan because the Herceptin the doctor had been administering for the past nine years was possibly causing heart damage.

I went on over to Daisy's for the night because I had surgery to have my gallbladder removed for the following morning. The next morning, I went in for surgery with Cody, who had directions for taking me home. His dad came and stayed at the hospital with him during the surgery and helped him get the car to the door. He was only fourteen and still on a permit, but he had driven me enough that I felt safe with him driving me home. I had the surgery by laparoscope, and so I only had three small incisions. I got up and went to work the next day. I then had to run back to Boise the next day for my MUGA scan to check on my heart. Then I had to rush home to waitress the next three days.

Daisy called to ask if I realized that my mom had defriended both of us on Facebook. It was the final straw, and I realized I no longer desired to be a part of either of my parents' lives. There was just too much pain associated with trying to love them, and I was exhausted from trying. I started to have an identity crisis and felt lost, except during the mornings when I spent time in prayer.

The results of the MUGA scan showed an output of 47 percent, normal being between 50 and 70 percent, so I now had a damaged, sluggish heart to deal with. It wasn't squeezing down as much, so the blood wasn't getting circulated through my system as needed. One day in July, I was sitting outside, thinking about Aponi, and hurting deeply when all of a sudden, I felt I was pulled through this tunnel, and on the other side, everything was just so quiet. A butterfly started flying around me and then over to the flowers and back to me. Then a bunch of butterflies appeared on the flowers, and two hummingbirds were chasing each other so close I could have reached out and touched them. I could not take my eyes off the one monarch fluttering back and forth. I kept hearing, "Aponi is all right," over and over until it finally sunk in. I thought this experience lasted about fifteen minutes, but when Cody asked where I had been after I went into the house, I discovered I had been out there in that trance for over two hours.

I had learned to cling to the Lord as my lifeline and trust Him for all my needs, but I still felt like I was drowning and that the water just kept splashing just above my head. I had always been against getting a tattoo, but after this butterfly experience, I felt an overwhelming need to research the meaning of butterfly tattoos and lilies online. I found that people believe the butterfly is a symbol of transformation and keeping our faith, and it's also associated with the soul. The lily symbolizes that the soul of the departed has received restored innocence after death. It came to me then that I needed to cover my physical scars with tattoos that would also help me deal with the emotional scars and somehow incorporate the monarch butterfly and orange lily. The title *Hidden Scars* came to me at this time, and I felt the overwhelming need to write my story and share with others. I also felt Christ suffered His scars for my soul, and so I came up with the subtitle, *Tattoos on the Soul*.

CHAPTER 26

THE DARKEST HOURS

You are my lamp, O Lord; the Lord turns my darkness into light.
—2 Samuel 22:29

Because of my heart condition, I could not walk very long without becoming light-headed, and I started gaining weight and felt the need to get away desperately. At the end of the month, I signed Cody up for a BMX park competition in San Diego. I stopped off at the surgeon for a post-op visit, and he informed me that my gallbladder had definitely been a problem for some time and that it was a good thing I had had it removed. As we made plans, I decided to swing through Twenty-nine Palms to get Broc and take him with us for the weekend. All I could think of was seeing a sunset on the beach. Two days on the road, and we picked Broc up and got to Oceanside after dark. I was too exhausted to do anything, so I sent the kids to get food. The next day, we went to the beach all day while Cody played in the ocean and then found a bike park where he could practice. We made it back to the beach for the sunset, and it was everything I had been craving. It was so God-inspired. I took so many pictures as the sun disappeared and felt a peace I had not felt in a very long time. I was not "lost" after all and knew I just needed to stay connected to the Lord. Because of my health issues, I live my life differently than most people by living and exploring for the moment, making as many memories for my kids as I can . . . while I can.

School started up, and I continued to go to the cardiologist. My first visit had the EKG showing abnormal results, so the doctor started me on blood pressure meds and beta blockers. I had to start at a low dose, and he wanted to double it every two weeks until we got to the desired amount; however, he didn't hold out any hope of getting me to the desired dosage without my heart rate dropping below fifty beats per minute, which would be in a danger zone. I adapted well the first two doublings but then started to get exhausted the next doublings, so we had to stretch the next doubling out to four weeks.

My eyes continued to cause problems with contacts, so I finally gave up and just started wearing bifocals all the time. I no longer recognized the person in the mirror. I had aged so much, and my appearance had changed so drastically in the last five months. I wasn't sure if I would ever make it completely back, but I was learning more and more to just trust the Lord. I thank Him daily for my children and grandbaby and all the family and friends He blesses me with. I know with Him, I will never be alone, and He will bring me through whatever comes my way.

I was told by both my oncologist and cardiologist that if I quit the Herceptin infusion treatment, I would die, even if it is to blame for my weakened heart. They knew the Adriamycin chemo I had had thirteen years prior was known to cause heart problems seven to eight years out, and the cardiologist noted that where the radiation was done on the left chest wall, there was no way my heart could have been avoided. Studies were showing that patients who were twelve years out were showing heart problems. My heart had taken a triple whammy, and I knew I was stuck between a rock and a hard place; however, I also knew God would bring me through. In October, I just kept crying, and I had the urge to just pull away from everyone and hide out at the house. I felt like I was on the edge of darkness that I would never be able to return from and was desperately clinging to God's light. That dark cloud had finally settled over my life, and I had no idea if I was going to make it through the storm. I had gotten away from going to church because I had moved and because I was waitressing on Sundays, and the Wednesday night Bible study group had fallen apart during the summer. Then a lady from our group called and wanted to start the Wednesday night Bible study again. We were all feeling Satan hammering at our doors, and we knew if we start meeting again, we would fare much better.

I decided to load Cody up and take him to his dream place, which is Tehachapi, California, for Camp Woodward West so that he could ride his bike. We needed the time together, so we pulled out on Thursday and took two days to get there. He rode for three days, and then we loaded back up and drove straight home. It wasn't until we were almost home before he finally started talking with me and bonding.

Cheer practice started in November, and I attempted to work out with them as I always had done. It worked at first, but then when I hit my final dose increase of heart meds and as I struggled with raising a teenage boy, I became too exhausted to participate. I felt like I was going under and could no longer breathe, and at my doctor's appointment, I told him that for first time ever I didn't care anymore. He looked stunned because I had always told him that I would fight until I drew my last breath, and now I was sitting here telling him I didn't care.

I wanted to give up and go home to the Lord, and then one morning on Veterans Day, after I have been fighting these illnesses for fifteen years, I just did not want to get out of bed anymore. I was done fighting, and as I lay there, I heard, "Get up, Tessa."

I replied, "God, I am done. I don't want to do this anymore."

And then the voice said in a more stern voice, "Get up, Tessa."

I continued to argue like a child refusing to get out of bed, but He was persistent. I told Him I could no longer do it, that I no longer had the strength or courage to fight, and that I missed my baby sister immensely, but He reminded me that though I was weak, I am made strong through Him. From praying constantly for His intervention here, He was making me get out of bed. When I hear God, it is not a verbal conversation that anyone can hear but more a feeling upon my heart of His Word. I got out of bed, showered, and attended the school's Veterans Day celebration; however, when the band started playing "Taps," the tears slipped unhindered down my cheeks, and I hurried home and crawled back into bed, begging the Lord to just please take me home. The pain was unbearable. I had heard "Taps" at two funerals this year, one being my baby sister's.

We spent Thanksgiving at Daisy's, and I ran and got Allen for the day. Allen and I started the oven on fire while taking the turkey out of the oven by splashing grease everywhere. We had the smoke alarms all going off, but it was a happy time for the kids even though my hair and eyebrows were singed. Then my kids all came home on Christmas day, and I was renewed with thankfulness for my blessings. I know though I am weak, I am made strong with the Lord. I will continue this battle in thankfulness; for I have gotten to watch my children grow up to be wonderful adults. My heart may have been broken and limping along, but it will learn to sing a happy tune again.

I was at treatment right before Christmas and hoping the year would just end. It had been hard, and financially, I was just barely hanging on. The MSTI nurses told me they had something for me, and after my treatment, they came out with three bags of groceries and gifts for me. I started to cry. I was just overwhelmed by the sheer beauty of these people's hearts. MSTI nurses are my angels, and I am in awe when I watch them work.

I have failed at every adult relationship I have ever had. Now I roll over and realize three of my kids are adults, and it starts to terrify me that I am going to do something to make them hate me. One thing is for certain: Life goes on, whether I am here or not. Wounds turn to scars, and through Jesus, I am healed.

CHAPTER 27

TRANSFORMATION

Do not conform any longer to the pattern of this world, but be transformed by the renewing of your mind. Then you will be able to test and approve what God's will is—his good, pleasing and perfect will.

—Romans 12:2

Three months after I was on the heart medications, I had an echocardiogram with results showing my heart output at 60 percent. The doctors had only hoped for 50 percent. Although my heart rate will always be low and I will always be on the medications, my heart is safe for now. I then visited my eye doctor, who decided to try daily-wear contact lenses, and they seemed to not bother my eyes. Until my immune system flares back up and attacks my eyes, I will wear the contacts. I decided it was time for the tattoo over my scars so I could truly move forward with life.

My vision of tattoo parlors has always been one of barred windows and triple-X atmosphere, and so when I pulled up to the parlor where I wished to have the tattoos done, I was sweating and suffering from anxiety before I even got out of the car. As I walked through the door of the Talon Tattoo Parlor in Boise, I was amazed at the well-lit room and the cleanliness of the place. I spotted Selena right off the bat and went to the counter to explain why I was there. Selena is the daughter of Maria, the lady who rallied the church to feed my family during the first three months of chemotherapy thirteen years prior.

I had no idea what I wanted for the tattoos over my scars but knew I needed a monarch butterfly to represent my baby sis. Selena, and I went into the restroom for privacy while I took off my shirt to show her the scars. Selena noted I had all three types of scars and was concerned about whether a specific one would hold the ink or not. After she measured and discussed the tattoos, she started sketching designs and asked if she could make a lily missing a petal and have the butterfly on the petal. I got goose bumps and asked how many petals a Lily had. I teared up when Selena said six because that would represent us six siblings with the one missing, the butterfly representing my baby sis. I made an appointment for a few weeks out in case I changed my mind and left.

The night before my appointment, I knew that I could not do this alone, so I texted my childhood friend Angel to see if she could come support me. Angel met me at the parlor the next day and visited with us for a few hours before she had to leave. The tattoos took six hours, and thankfully, I felt very little pain because of all the missing nerves from the surgeries. I talked to Selena the remainder of the time and knew I had to find Maria and have this whole thing come full circle. Selena told me that now the breast cancer patients have their nipple attached to their hip until the reconstruction is complete, and then the doctors can reattach the women's own nipples. I later found Maria on Facebook and left her a message. I am waiting for the day I can visit with her face-to-face.

Although I didn't wish for this cancer, I look at it as a gift because it changed my life. I have met so many beautiful people because of it and have been humbled so many times. I have learned to walk with the Lord. I don't start my days without prayer time, and I have come to rely solely on Him for my provisions. I may not have all I want, but He has always given me all I have ever needed.

In May, I took off on one of my adventures and drove to Texas so that I could spend the week with Faith and her family and then attend Lilly's college graduation. We knew it would be difficult because we were right at a year since we had lost Aponi. My mom flew down with Hope, and we met up the morning of the graduation at the hotel and then followed one another to the campus. After Lilly received her diploma, everyone left except for Faith, her husband, Hope, and me. Another hour later and graduation over, we headed back to the hotel to celebrate. My mom had been drinking by the time I got there, but everyone enjoyed telling stories about Lilly and then eating. I was getting ready to leave because I was headed out to meet a friend in Tulsa, and as I turned around, my mom was standing in my path with her arms crossed and looking at me challengingly. I was not going to ruin Lilly's day, and because I had my purse and laptop in my left hand, I hugged her with my right arm; however, instead of hugging me back, she grabbed my wrist and pulled me front and center. I told her not to even go there and pulled away. I ended up stumbling out of the hotel, fighting an emotional breakdown, not even getting to hug my sister good-bye. Lilly and Hope followed me out, and I was able to pull it together after a bit and drove off.

After I spent the night in Tulsa and visited an old friend, I drove on to Indianapolis to surprise Merry. I hadn't seen her since John was a baby and felt the need to see her. I spent two days there before I headed home. This trip gave me the time alone in a car to go over my relationships and what I needed to do. My parents had always gotten a fight out of me, and I was no longer participating. I realized that I was doing to my son, Cody, exactly what they had done to me my whole life. I knew I needed to change things now, or he would leave home hating me. I made a decision to love my parents from a distance. Allen had now gotten a house and was working and slowly rebuilding his life, although he was not contributing financially toward the raising of his children. I was going to figure out how to be civil to him as well. My children would not have to choose between us ever again.

The tattoos covered my physical scars, but they also did something deeper to my heart as well. I know that my soul will be okay. I keep my eyes on the prize of eternity with the Lord and will live in joy and expectation of that time with one breath at a time.

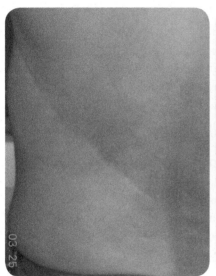

The scar is from reconstructive surgery where the muscle on the left side was brought around to help form the left breast. The tattoo covering that same scar with the lily that represents myself and four of my siblings, a petal for each of us and one missing for my baby sis.

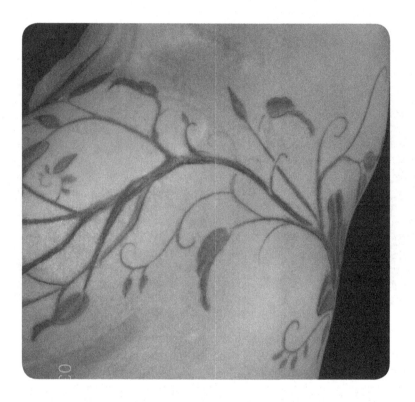

The branches and Lily wrap around my left side just under my armpit. The scar from the lymph node removal is untouched as is the scar under the breast.

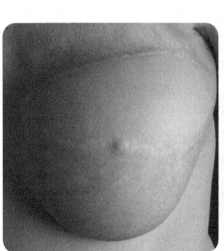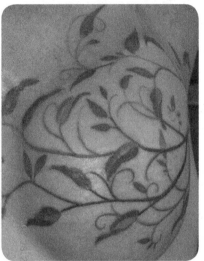

The left breast before and after tattooing over the scars. The upper part on the left picture is my back muscle and skin. The nub is the result of a failed attempt at surgically creating a nipple. This is muscle expanded out to form a pocket, and then an implant is replaced.

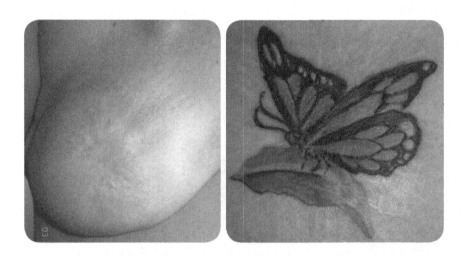

This is my right breast where the nipple and breast tissue had been removed, the muscle expanded out, and then replaced with an implant.

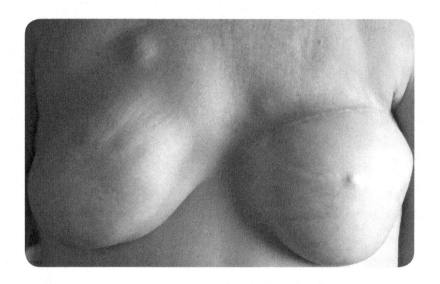

The way I looked for twelve years.

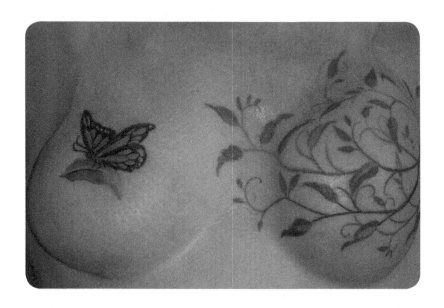

After tattooing. The butterfly represents my baby sis, and she is on the missing petal from the lily. I hope in the future to have a little more work done to make it look as if the butterfly and petal are floating in the wind.